# NEGOTIATING AND INFLUENCING SKILLS

*This book is dedicated
to all the peacemakers and
peacekeepers in the world,
and on a more personal level to
my Aunt Irene Wade
and to my children, Andrew
and Kathryn McRae.*

# NEGOTIATING AND INFLUENCING SKILLS

## The Art of Creating and Claiming Value

## Brad McRae

SAGE Publications
*International Educational and Professional Publisher*
Thousand Oaks   London   New Delhi

*For information:*

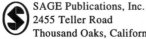

SAGE Publications, Inc.
2455 Teller Road
Thousand Oaks, California 91320
E-mail: order@sagepub.com

SAGE Publications Ltd.
6 Bonhill Street
London EC2A 4PU
United Kingdom

SAGE Publications India Pvt. Ltd.
M-32 Market
Greater Kailash I
New Delhi 110 048 India

Printed in the United States of America

*Library of Congress Cataloging-in-Publication Data*

McRae, Brad.
    Negotiating and influencing skills: The art of creating and
claiming value / by Brad McRae.
        p.  cm.
    Includes bibliographical references and index.
    ISBN 0-7619-1184-7 (cloth: alk. paper). — ISBN 0-7619-1185-5
(pbk.: alk. paper)
    1. Negotiation. 2. Influence (Psychology)  I. Title.
BF637.N4M39  1997
158'.5—dc21                                                          97-21051

This book is printed on acid-free paper.

98  99  00  01  02  03  04  7  6  5  4  3  2  1

*Acquisitions Editor:* Marquita Flemming
*Editorial Assistant:* Frances Borghi
*Production Editor:* Sanford Robinson
*Copy Editor:* Joyce Kuhn
*Production Assistant:* Karen Wiley
*Typesetter/Designer:* Christina Hill/Rebecca Evans
*Cover Designer:* Candice Harman
*Print Buyer:* Anna Chin

# Contents

■ ■ ■ ■

## 1. Introduction

*This chapter examines why negotiating and influencing skills are challenging to learn and how the concepts of "Powerful Questions," "Salient Feedback," and the "Ladder of Knowledge" can help you learn these critically important skills. A survey on negotiation is then presented to help you assess the role that negotiation skills play in both your personal and professional life.*

## 2. Creating and Claiming Value

*This chapter introduces you to the two most important elements in all negotiations: creating value and claiming value. You will learn how to assess your own skills in these two important areas and learn how to better monitor your success in future negotiations. The chapter then looks at the role of ethical decision making in the*

*negotiating process and the importance of your reputation as a*
*negotiator and concludes by looking at the styles and characteristics*
*of highly effective negotiators and their less effective counterparts.*

## 3. Assessing Your Current Negotiating Style

*How well you create and claim value depends on how well your*
*negotiating skills have been developed. It also depends on how*
*well those skills are integrated into a cohesive negotiating style. The*
*purpose of this chapter is to help you examine your current abilities*
*as a negotiator and to formulate a list of ways you would like to*
*improve them. A seminal study is presented that looks at the eight*
*critical differences between effective senior managers and their*
*average counterparts. You are then invited to rate your ability*
*on each of these eight characteristics. You will also learn about a*
*strategy designed to help you use the power of salient feedback to*
*assess how others see your current negotiating strengths and to*
*examine areas where improvement is desirable.*

## 4. Principles and Techniques for Creating and Claiming Value

*This chapter explains the 10 essential differences between effective*
*negotiators and their ineffective counterparts and then introduces*
*you to the critical importance of BATNA (Best Alternative to a*
*Negotiated Agreement) and muscle level (i.e., how much power you*
*need to bring to the negotiating table). The chapter discusses several*
*techniques to get stalled negotiations back on track and then exam-*
*ines the strategic role of "frames" in helping you become more*
*persuasive and the critical role of "precedent setting" in the*
*negotiating process.*

## 5. Dealing With Difficult People and Difficult Situations

*Difficult people and difficult situations are a true test of your*
*negotiating and influencing skills. They also provide you with one*
*of the best sources of information on what you need to do differ-*
*ently to negotiate more effectively. This chapter examines the eight*
*critical skills needed to successfully negotiate with difficult people*
*or in difficult situations.*

## 6. Developing Higher-Order Skills

*This chapter explores the development of higher-order negotiating skills, looks at the development of individual skills and subskills using the "P.R.I.C.E." method, and explores the value of learning from interviews with experienced negotiators and learning from mentors. As your negotiating skills must work together congruently and harmoniously if you are to be a truly effective negotiator, the chapter concludes with five techniques for putting all these skills together to create an effective, integrated whole.*

## 7. The Power of Commitment

*This chapter explores the power of commitment in the negotiating process and also affords you the opportunity to examine a long-term contentious negotiation from start to finish. The case involves the building of coalitions, the increase of muscle level, and the power of using objective criteria and external standards. The chapter centers on a child injury case and the use of the elements of the "Getting to Yes" model to negotiate a resolution based on "principle."*

## 8. Conclusion

*Learning effective negotiating and influencing skills is a life-long process. In a very real sense, reading this book is only the beginning point in that process. To answer the question "Where do I go from here?" several suggestions are presented in this chapter regarding books to read, courses to take, and the continuing use of the feedback forms provided in this book. Information also is presented on programs that teach negotiating and influencing skills in elementary schools and high schools.*

# Preface

■ ■ ■ ■

One of the most useful descriptions of the process of negotiation I have found is that "a negotiation is taking place any time two people are communicating, where one or both parties have a goal in mind." For example, my wife and I want to go to the movies Saturday night. She wants to see movie "X," and I want to see movie "Y." Using this broad definition of negotiating, most of us spend at least 50% of our time negotiating. This is a whopping amount of time.

If we spend this much time negotiating, why aren't we all better at it? The answer is that most of us have had very little formal training in how to improve our negotiating and influencing skills. The good news is that there are more courses available to the public and to businesses and organizations to improve negotiating skills than there were in the past. Beside the negotiation courses currently offered, many excellent books have been written to help us learn negotiating and influencing skills. However, I feel that there is an area that has not been fully addressed by any of these books. This need could be filled by a text or workbook that would aid you, the reader, in acquiring the skills necessary to be an effective negotiator. How to acquire these skills is the focus of this book.

The research on transfer of training has found that less than 10% of theory and skills taught in training courses is transferred to the work setting. One would surmise that reading a book—generally speaking, a much more passive approach to learning—would offer much less of an opportunity to transfer the training that one has learned.

For this reason, the emphasis in this book is on practical application of negotiation skills. This book is designed to be highly interactive. It contains many exercises that have been carefully constructed to help you develop and broaden your negotiation style, to become more flexible and fluid in approach, to try out new strategies and techniques, and to observe the results. By actively involving yourself in these exercises, you can watch your skills improve.

This book presents a two-step process toward the mastery of negotiating and influencing skills: first, *development of skills* by means of interactive exercises, and second, *transfer of training* by applying the negotiating skills you are learning to your life at home and at work.

# Acknowledgments

■　■　■　■

Many people have contributed significantly to the creation of this book. Through courses at the Harvard Program on Negotiation, I have been able to learn from Roger Fisher, William Ury, Lawrence Susskind, Bruce Patton, and Jeffrey Rubin, all of whom have influenced my thinking on negotiation more than they will ever know. I also thank my corporate clients. Being able to teach negotiation skills throughout such organizations as Maritime Telephone & Telegraph; Nova Scotia Power Corporation; St. Mary's University at the World Trade Center; LASMO Nova Scotia; Co-Op Atlantic; Michelin Canada; Honda Canada; the governments of Canada, Nova Scotia, and New Brunswick; and in the United States, Mexico and Africa provided me with the opportunity to learn about the kinds of negotiations that take place in a number of different institutions and organizations and to learn where the theory of Principled Negotiation works and how it must be modified to meet the specific circumstances of each particular situation.

I thank my colleagues Claudine Lowry, Carol Hill, Marilyn MacMullin, Mike Whitehouse, and Shauna Shirley for their careful reading of this manuscript and for their insightful suggestions regarding both the context and the style of this book. I also thank Diane Metzger, my office manager and editor, without whose help and encouragement this manuscript would have remained partially written forever.

Help, help, and more help with my long overdue computer upgrade and translation of the manuscript to a modern word processing program was generously provided by Bruce Whynott, Peter Lynch, and Ho. In turning the manuscript into a book, I was greatly assisted by my editor Marquita Flemming, her assistant Frances Borghi, senior production editor Sanford Robinson, and all the staff at Sage. Their professional guidance and personal encouragement were invaluable.

Last, I thank my wife, Lynn Crosby, and my children, Andrew and Katie, and our nanny and friend, Marilyn Christie, for their support and understanding throughout the research, writing, and editing and rere-searching, rewriting, and reediting of this manuscript.

# Introduction

## ▦ Negotiating and Influencing Skills Are Important to Learn

In my experience in teaching negotiating skills, I have found that most people misunderstand the word *negotiating*. Many people assume that negotiating skills are only used in the context of labor/management negotiations. I see this differently: Negotiating and influencing skills apply in every area of our work and our personal lives. We constantly negotiate. We negotiate agreements, and agreements are what make relationships work. We also negotiate to solve problems, and we negotiate to resolve conflicts. The purpose of this book is to help you become a better interpersonal negotiator—whether the other party in the negotiation is your employer, subordinate, coworker, spouse, parent, child, or neighbor. In spite of people's misunderstanding of the topic, I did not want to drop the word *negotiating* from the title of the course because negotiating is exactly what we need to learn. After we better understand the process, we become less intimidated by the term *negotiating*.

A number of years ago, I realized that the focus of the course I taught involved more than just negotiating skills. Therefore, I changed the name of the course to "Effective Negotiating and Influencing Skills." For the sake of brevity, in this book the term *negotiating* can be understood as incorporating both negotiating and influencing skills. As you can see, negotiating is defined quite broadly in this book. In fact, the definition that I prefer is this: "A negotiation takes place any time two or more people are communicating, and at least one of those persons has a goal in mind."

Negotiation skills are important because we spend a great deal of time negotiating. Research shows that most managers and supervisors spend up to 50% of their time negotiating. Salespeople, project managers, civil servants, engineers, technicians, medical personnel, and people working in the service industry, among others, also spend a great deal of their time negotiating. The outcomes of these negotiations determine our success in both our professional and our personal lives. Or as Gary Karrass, a noted speaker on negotiating skills, states, "We don't get what we want in this life, we get what we negotiate."

## ■ Negotiating and Influencing Skills Are Difficult to Learn

Why are negotiating skills so difficult to learn? There are three primary reasons:

- ■ The first reason has to do with the complexity of the negotiating process. Negotiating and influencing skills are a complex network of interacting skills. One can think of negotiating and influencing skills as a symphony orchestra of skills. Each instrument (subskill) must be used together with all the others in a harmonious and congruent manner. If one instrument (subskill) is off, the whole orchestra will be off—in other words, the negotiation will not turn out as well as it otherwise could have.

- ■ The second reason why negotiating is difficult to learn has to do with timing. In the real estate field, it is said that there are three important factors: location, location, and location. In negotiating, also, it has been said that there are three important factors: timing, timing, and timing. The step that you take at Stage 1 in the negotiation to effectively bring about movement toward resolution will, if employed at Step 10, cause the negotiation to break off or escalate into a conflict.

Traditional Learning Curve

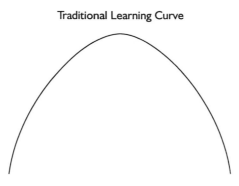

**Figure 1.1**   Traditional Learning Curve

▦ The third reason why negotiating is difficult to learn is because negotiations are made up of two seemingly paradoxical skill sets: CREATING VALUE and CLAIMING VALUE.

*Creating value.* We create value by listening very carefully to the other person's needs and interests. We patiently help our partner to learn what are our needs and interests. We look for ways to integrate and/or link these interests together. We look for and/or invent creative options that meet both parties' interests. We create value by expanding the pie.

*Claiming value.* We claim value when we get our needs and interests met. We claim value by being well prepared and by being assertive. We can also claim value by being aggressive, by being dishonest, by deceiving, by bullying, and by using dirty tricks. Balancing the negotiating activities of creating value and claiming value is the essential task of all negotiators. Effective negotiators are equally effective at both of these skills. An in-depth examination of creating value and claiming value is the focus of Chapter 3.

If it is true that negotiating and influencing skills are difficult to learn, how can we approach this important task? Some fundamental tools can help adults learn more effectively:

▦ Powerful questions
▦ Salient feedback
▦ The ladder of knowledge

Enhanced Learning Curve

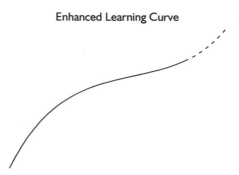

**Figure 1.2**    Enhanced Learning Curve

The learning curve for most courses and for most books looks like the curve in Figure 1.1.

Three months later, the course or the book has made little, if any, difference. By contrast, consider the curve in Figure 1.2, in which the learning continues after the course has finished or after the book has been read.

Two essential factors must be met to produce this type of learning curve: powerful questions and salient feedback.

### Powerful Questions

I was introduced to the idea of powerful questions at the Dalhousie University Killiam Lecture Series. The fund for the Killiam Lecture Series, which honors the memory of one of its greatest benefactors, enables the university to bring in three world-class lecturers for three consecutive Thursday evenings each October. Each series has a theme, such as "The Environment," "Space," "War," or "The Women's Movement." In 1991, the topic for the series was the USSR, which was most timely, as the Soviet Union was in the process of disintegrating. The second lecturer of the series was a man named Marshall Goldman, who had written a biography of Mikhail Gorbachev. Near the end of his lecture, Mr. Goldman talked about the concept of powerful questions, and he illustrated it with this question: Why did Gorbachev do what he did in initiating *perestroika*?

Goldberg said that in order to answer that question we have to go back 30 years to a time when, as a young man, Gorbachev was walking on the beach in the Crimea with his buddy Chervenatchki. They talked about their grandfathers and discovered that, although according to family lore their grandfathers were very good and very honorable men, they had been killed in the Stalinist purges. Gorbachev later met and married Raisa, and he learned from her that both of her grandfathers also were killed in the Stalinist purges. At that time, Gorbachev started to ask himself the following powerful question: "How could a moral form of government go around killing off everyone's grandfathers?" He thought about this question for a very long time and finally realized that it couldn't—and therefore, the form of government had to change. Many years later, as prime minister of the USSR, he introduced perestroika. From this lecture, the concept that powerful questions bring about powerful results was planted firmly in my mind.

The powerful questions that I ask the students in my negotiation course to think about are the following:

- "What is my style of reaching agreements with others?" To arrive at your answer, you may want to consider this question: "When does my style work for me, and when does it work against me?"
- "How do I have to become more skillful, fluid, and flexible in my negotiating style so that it will work for me in a greater number of situations, thereby increasing my ability to accomplish my personal goals and also the goals of my team or department, and of the company or organization for which I work?"
- "What is my shadow style?" For example, John's preferred style is to be warm, open, and congenial, but his shadow style may be quite aggressive when he is tired or when he has strong feelings about a particular negotiation. Our shadow style can be responsible for breaking off, giving in, or escalating a conflict. It is important not only to improve our primary style but to better control our shadow or secondary style. More will be said about how to control ourselves during the negotiation process in Chapter 5, "Dealing With Difficult People."

## Salient Feedback

Salient feedback is feedback that is so personally meaningful that it makes it much more likely that we will change our behavior. Medical research conducted in Vancouver helps make clear the idea behind salient feedback.

In this particular study, a group of women, all of whom were three months' pregnant, were assigned randomly to Group A and Group B, which helped ensure that the two groups were statistically equal before the experiment. All participants in the study filled out an anonymous questionnaire regarding their caffeine and alcohol consumption and their use of nonprescription illegal drugs. Before the experiment, both groups were equal on these measures. Then all participants were given an ultrasound examination, after which a technician told each of them that their fetus was developing normally. (Only women whose fetuses were developing normally were used in the study.) The only difference in treatment of the two groups was that Group A participants were given the information verbally, whereas Group B participants were also allowed to look at their fetuses on the ultrasound screen for 30 seconds.

Three months later, the women in both groups were again given the anonymous questionnaire. The experimenters were trying to answer the following question: Would the women in the two groups be similar or different?

During the first trimester of their pregnancy, these women already had received a great deal of feedback that things were different than before pregnancy. Building a placenta during the first trimester is like climbing a mountain 24 hours a day; added to that are hormonal changes and morning sickness. This amounts to a great deal of feedback that things in these women's lives were radically different than they had been previous to pregnancy. Would 30 seconds of visual feedback make a difference? The answer is yes. The women who saw their babies significantly reduced their intake of caffeine, alcohol, and drugs. Why was this 30 seconds of visual feedback so powerful? The reason was that, as the old saying goes, "seeing is believing!"

To make the idea of salient feedback work for you, ideas will be suggested in this book to help you obtain personally meaningful feedback on your negotiating and influencing style.

**The Ladder of Knowledge**

The ladder of knowledge postulates that there are four levels of knowledge. The first level is *information*. At this level, we intellectually understand how to perform a certain skill; for example, we know the difference on an intellectual level between being aggressive and being assertive. However, we do not know how to be assertive in real life. That comes at the second level, which is called *knowledge*. At this level, we understand the skill intellectually and know how to perform it. However, we have to know when and when not to be assertive. For example, you understand how to be assertive with your spouse about keeping the house cleaner, and you also know that your spouse is having a difficult time at work and that this is not the time to use your assertiveness skills. This is the level of *judgment*. The last level is that of *wisdom*. At this level, you use the right combination of skills at the right time with the right people and in the proper context, which considers the relationship's history, where that relationship is at the present time, and how you would like it to develop in the future. Applying these concepts to the development of negotiating and influencing skills is the purpose of this book.

## Information

At this level, we broaden our understanding of the process of negotiating and learn about different tools that may be of use to us. We also learn a richer and more precise language to describe the negotiating process. We learn more advanced concepts, like "muscle level," "choice points," "creating value," and "claiming value." We learn concepts like BATNA (Best Alternative to a Negotiated Agreement) (Fisher & Ury, 1981). We can describe different styles of negotiation; however, we may not be able to negotiate any more effectively than we could have before we acquired this information. It is like reading a book about tennis: Doing so does not necessarily, by itself, mean that one can play tennis any better.

## Knowledge

At this level, we have developed both skills and awareness. One begins to be able not only to describe the skill in question but to perform the skill. For example, it is one thing to be able to describe to a friend what one would do in asking one's boss for a raise. It is something altogether different to be able to effectively negotiate that raise.

At this level, we also begin to become aware that we have choices in how we respond to certain situations. This increased awareness and the skill give us knowledge.

There are many books on how to negotiate. Very few, if any of them, combine negotiating skills with the principles of adult learning. The purpose of this book is to help you better understand how to learn negotiating and influencing skills and to provide exercises that will facilitate the acquisition of these important skills.

## ▨ Judgment

Judgment is the ability to use the right skill at the right time. Learning judgment is partly a trial-and-error process. Although we can shorten the time it takes to learn judgment by reading about negotiating and by watching expert negotiators, it will still take some trial-and-error learning for all of us to become more proficient negotiators. Based on the interviews I conducted with expert negotiators, this book provides you with a better understanding of the importance of timing and judgment. The book also provides exercises to help you recover as quickly as possible from mistakes and to learn all that you can from each negotiating experience.

## ▨ Wisdom

Wisdom comes from an in-depth integration of our information, knowledge, and judgment. With wisdom, we are better able to negotiate good outcomes, to negotiate a good process by which these outcomes are derived, and to negotiate precedents that we can be proud of.

As we move up the ladder of knowledge, we need to make better decisions about both when and how to negotiate. In fact, negotiating can be looked upon as interactive decision making—that is, two or more people trying individually and collectively to make the best decision possible regarding the outcome of the negotiation. Therefore, it makes sense to look closely at the process of decision making in negotiations. There are three styles of decision making: nonvigilant, hypervigilant, and vigilant.

A *nonvigilant* decision is one that needs to be made but we don't see it, or if we see it we don't act on it. As an example, I live with my family in an old Victorian house. One day, five years ago, I noticed a small leak in the back part of the roof. It only leaked when the wind was blowing very hard from the west, and so I ignored the leak. Five years ago, this would have cost $600 to repair. Last week, the repair was estimated at $1,600. I had made a nonvigilant decision about fixing the roof on my home.

People make nonvigilant decisions about keeping an old car running, which eventually costs them a fortune, or staying in a relationship with a friend long after the friendship has died. Some of the nonvigilant types of decisions we can make vis-à-vis negotiating is to not realize that we are negotiating, to go into the negotiation underprepared, and not to take a break from the negotiation when we need to. At the opposite extreme from nonvigilant decisions are hypervigilant decisions.

A *hypervigilant* decision is made when a person panics and acts on the first decision that he or she thinks of, without considering appropriate alternatives. For example, a group of patrons are in a movie theater when it catches fire. There is widespread panic, and people stampede toward the main doors, which are blocked by the fire. Hundreds of lives are lost unnecessarily because no one looked around to see that there were exits behind the movie screen. The movie patrons made a hypervigilant decision because they did not take time to fully explore all their options.

A *vigilant* decision is the type we want to make more often. Vigilant decisions take into account the best information, processed in the best way, to produce optimum results. For example, 10 years ago a passenger by the name of Bill was returning from a vacation in Florida to his home in New England. Bill was seated in row 24 of a DC-9, just opposite the washroom in the rear of the plane. About an hour after take-off, Bill saw smoke coming out of the restroom and called the flight attendant. When the flight attendant opened the door, flames could be seen, and the passenger compartment started filling up with black, toxic smoke.

Bill realized that the plane would have to land soon and by that time it would be filled with smoke. The plane made an emergency landing in a wheat field. Although Bill was very frightened, he did not panic. He put a handkerchief over his face, got down on his hands and knees, and crawled toward the exit in row 12, carefully counting the rows as he passed them—1, 2, 3, 4, and so on. He then turned to the right, crawled out onto the wing of the plane, and escaped safely. If Bill had panicked and miscounted, he might not have made it out of the plane. The purpose of this book is to help us all make better, more vigilant decisions regarding the outcomes reached by the process of negotiating, to make better decisions about the process we use in reaching those outcomes, and to develop better precedents for future negotiations.

You are reading this book because you want to be a better negotiator. An excellent way to start this process is to fill out the following Negotiation Survey.

▓  ▓  ▓  ▓

## EXERCISE 1.1
### Negotiation Survey

1. Estimate the percentage of time you spend negotiating on your job, with "negotiating" being defined quite broadly. The definition I prefer is that a negotiation is any communication between people in which one or both parties has a goal in mind. For instance, if you were communicating with an employee about arriving at the job on time, that communication is defined as a negotiation. With this definition in mind, estimate the percentage of time, from 0% to 99%, that you spend negotiating at work: _____.

2. Rate your effectiveness as a negotiator at work on a scale from 1 to 10, where 1 is "very ineffective" and 10 is "very effective." For example, rating yourself a 1 could indicate that you give in on all of your interests to keep the peace or, alternatively, that you never back down and that most of your negotiations escalate into a fight. Rating yourself a 10 means that you possess the wisdom of Solomon and can successfully negotiate a flawless settlement for every conflict: _____.

3. What will be the biggest challenge facing you in your business/professional career in the coming year?

4. Rate your effectiveness as a negotiator in your personal life outside work on a scale from 1 to 10, where 1 is "very ineffective" and 10 is "very effective." Again, rating yourself a 1 could indicate that you give in on all of your interests to keep the peace or, alternatively, that you never back down and that most of your negotiations escalate into a fight. Rating

yourself a 10 means that you possess the wisdom of Solomon and can successfully negotiate a perfect settlement for every conflict: _____.

5. What will be the biggest challenge facing you in your personal life in the coming year?

6. What would you like to learn or how would you like to be able to negotiate differently as a result of reading this book and improving your own negotiating skills?

7. What advantages would accrue to you from becoming a better negotiator?

8. What advantages would accrue to your company or organization from your becoming a better negotiator?

※ ※ ※ ※

You can now compare your responses to these questions to the averages of hundreds of respondents who have participated in my negotiation courses. These respondents estimated that the average amount of time that they spent negotiating is 50%, with "negotiating" being defined quite broadly. The average rating they gave for their negotiating effectiveness was 5 on the 10-point scale.

Among the advantages to learning how to negotiate more effectively are increased satisfaction in both your personal and your work life. Some of the benefits that my course participants have listed are these:

※ Less stress
※ Better business relationships
※ Better interpersonal relationships
※ More business successes

- More respect from others
- More self-respect
- Better networking
- Improved reputation
- Winning more contracts
- Successfully completing more contracts
- Dealing more effectively with difficult people
- More peace of mind
- Faster recovery from dealing with difficult people and difficult situations
- Better learning from experience
- Better understanding of others' needs and interests
- Saying "no" more frequently to unnecessary obligations I used to say "yes" to
- Better preparation for negotiations
- Developing more insight into other people's needs and interests
- Developing more creative solutions
- To become more persuasive
- To better understand my personal strengths and weaknesses as a negotiator
- Improving my ability to negotiate as a member of a team
- Increasing my efficiency at work
- Developing more options
- Knowing when to take a break from the negotiation
- Knowing when to focus on the negotiation process and when to focus on the substance of the negotiation
- Knowing when not to negotiate
- Reaching better solutions for all parties concerned
- To deal better with difficult, irate clients
- Better ability to get real commitments
- Developing more confidence in myself as a negotiator
- Better ability to find and expand common ground
- Developing more control/Feeling less intimidated when negotiating
- Improved comfort level and confidence
- Knowing when to confront and when not to confront
- To reach more goals with everyone committed
- When to walk away

We will now turn our attention to two of the most important negotiating skills—creating value and claiming value.

# Creating and Claiming Value

■ ■ ■ ■

This chapter introduces the two most important elements in all negotiations—creating value and claiming value. You will learn how to assess your own skills in these two important areas and learn how to better monitor your success in future negotiations. We then examine the role of moral decision making in the negotiating process and the importance of your reputation as a negotiator. The chapter concludes with a look at the styles and characteristics of highly effective negotiators and their less effective counterparts.

## ■ Creating Value

We create value by listening very carefully to the other person's needs and interests. We patiently help our partner learn what our needs and interests are. We look for ways to integrate and link these interests together. We look for and/or invent creative options that meet both parties' interests. We create value by expanding the pie. The following examples illustrate the concept of creating value.

After our son Andrew was born, my wife and I found ourselves in conflict on Sunday mornings. Lynn wanted to go swimming to increase her physical fitness and to help take off the weight she had gained during the pregnancy. I was working on a book on time management and wanted to spend Sunday mornings writing. We could have compromised, whereby she could swim for part of the morning and I could write for part of the morning, but I found that I needed bigger chunks of time for my writing. She could have gone swimming one week and I could have written the next, but she would not have been able to get into good enough shape to make the swimming worthwhile, and I needed to write more consistently to meet the deadline for the book contract.

The solution was to hire Laura to baby-sit. This created value for Lynn because she could swim every Sunday. It created value for me because I could write every Sunday. It created value for Laura because, although she had taken a course on how to baby-sit, she had never actually done it. Our house was the perfect opportunity for Laura to start baby-sitting, for I was upstairs available to help and supervise when needed. The experience created value for Laura. It also created value for Andrew. Having a break from child care meant that we were better and more attentive parents. This one solution met my wife's interests, my interests, the baby-sitter's interests, and the baby's interests. Value was thus created for four people.

In another example, the office space next door to me became available to rent. I wanted to expand, but there was much more space than I needed, and the cost was prohibitive. At the time, I was working part-time for myself and part-time as the regional manager for a national employee assistance company. We looked at sharing the space and the cost, but there was still more space than we both needed, and the cost was still prohibitive. The solution was to sublet part of the space to a third party at a low rent, with a six-month notice to vacate. The new space consisted of one large office, one small office, a storage area, and a waiting room. Now that we had the space (creating value), we then had to decide who would get the large office (claiming value).

## ▓ Claiming Value

We claim value when we get our needs and interests met. We claim value by being well prepared, by being assertive, by creating value that we can then claim. We can also claim value by being aggressive, by being dishonest, by deceiving, by bullying, and by using dirty tricks. Therefore, moral decision making is part of the negotiating process.

Most negotiators tend to be better at either creating value or claiming value. I learned this the hard way at the first course I took at the Harvard Project on Negotiation titled "Teaching Negotiation in the Organization." As part of the course, I did three negotiations with a fellow participant. Tom C. was the vice president in charge of sales for one of the large U.S. television networks. Tom was very experienced in multimillion-dollar negotiations, wore expensive suits, and looked like a halfback for a national football team. He was negotiating with Brad McRae, an inexperienced negotiator. As it turned out, I was better than Tom at creating value. My background in counseling gave me the listening skills to understand his interests. I also developed creative solutions that helped expand the pie. However, after the negotiation was over, I looked down at my tally sheet and saw that Tom had 98% of the pie. He was better at claiming value.

We entered into our second negotiation. Once again, I was better at creating value, and once again Tom took 98% of the pie. I was beginning to see that there was something radically wrong with my negotiating style.

We entered into our third negotiation. Once again, I was better at creating value. And I am proud to be able to tell you that at the end of that negotiation Tom only had 95% of the pie. The feedback was clear. I had to become more vigilant and more assertive about claiming value.

Creating and claiming value can be difficult concepts to grasp. Sometimes, the same skill can be used in creating value and in claiming value, and sometimes, you can create value and claim value at the same time.

Among the skills that are used to create and claim value are the following:

- Having a clear understanding of what your interests are when the negotiation begins
- Being prepared with relevant information prior to the process (i.e., doing your homework/research)
- Presenting your position clearly, being able to clarify it and justify it throughout
- Sticking to the issue and not attacking the person with whom you are negotiating

- Creating value requires the following skills:
  Openness
  Communication
  Active listening
  Asking high-yield questions
  Identifying interests
  Developing creative solutions
  Joint problem solving
  Preventing conflict escalation

- Claiming value requires the following skills:
  Preparation
  Developing a good BATNA
  Being assertive about one's interests
  Being persuasive
  Being a good presenter

- Claiming value can also include the following:
  Being aggressive
  Misleading
  Lying
  Advantageously shaping opponents' perceptions of the bargaining range

**Figure 2.1**  Skills Used in Creating and Claiming Value

- Listening to the other person's position respectfully, recognizing that they have valid points
- Trying to see the situation from the other person's perspective
- Brainstorming to create options and alternatives
- Looking at creative solutions to similar types of problems
- When it appears that you are in a deadlock, suggesting time away from the table to think about options
- Solving the problem with the help of a mediator

Figure 2.1 summarizes the skills involved in creating and claiming value.

The following exercise has been designed to help you get a better feel for creating and claiming value.

■ ■ ■ ■

**EXERCISE 2.1**
**Creating and Claiming Value**

1. Think of the last negotiation you were in. Summarize that negotiation in the space provided below:

2. Rate yourself from 1 to 10 on how well you created value in that negotiation, where 1 is "created little or no value" and 10 is "created a great deal of value."

My effectiveness in creating value in my last negotiation was: _____

3. Next, rate yourself from 1 to 10 on how well you claimed value in your last negotiation, where 1 represents "obtained little or no value for myself" and 10 represents "obtained a great deal of value for myself."

My effectiveness in claiming value in my last negotiation was: _____

The next step is to study how you create and claim value in your next three negotiations. This will help you determine your own pattern in creating and claiming value. To be an effective negotiator, you have to be good at both creating and claiming value. The following form has been designed to help you examine your own pattern of creating and claiming value.

**CREATING/CLAIMING VALUE FORM**

1. Briefly summarize a negotiation that you participated in.
   Rate your effectiveness in creating value (1-10):  _____
   Rate your effectiveness in claiming value (1-10):  _____

2. Briefly summarize another negotiation.
   Rate your effectiveness in creating value (1-10):  _____
   Rate your effectiveness in claiming value (1-10):  _____

3. Briefly summarize another negotiation.

   Rate your effectiveness in creating value (1-10):     _____

   Rate your effectiveness in claiming value (1-10):     _____

4. From your observations in these three negotiations, what do you do well in the area of creating value?

5. From your observations in these three negotiations, what specifically do you need to do to improve your skills in creating value?

6. From your observations in these three negotiations, what do you do well in the area of claiming value?

7. From your observations in these three negotiations, what specifically do you need to do to improve your skills in claiming value?

▓  ▓  ▓  ▓

The above exercise was designed to help you develop more awareness of the concepts of creating and claiming value and of your own particular skills in these two important areas, and it has encouraged you to look at ways to improve your skills in these two areas to become a more competent negotiator.

There is one more way you can use the concepts of creating and claiming value to improve your ability to negotiate. Instead of waiting until the end of the negotiation to rate yourself on creating and claiming value, take a break in the middle of the negotiation and rate yourself on these skills. This valuable mid-course assessment has the added advantage of helping you to make mid-course corrections while there is still time to modify the outcome of the negotiation.

## ▨  Claiming Value and Moral Decision Making

The following story, which first appeared in Bacow and Wheeler's (1984) book *Environmental Dispute Resolution,* can help you learn a great deal about (a) the importance of making assumptions and (b) the role of moral decision making in the negotiating process.

> Teddy Roosevelt was nearing the end of a hard-fought and very close election campaign. Critical to his success was a final whistle-stop journey through the heartland of America. At each stop, Roosevelt planned to inspire the citizens with oratory, and leave each with a small pamphlet, three million of which had been printed. On the cover was a stern "Presidential" portrait; inside was a stirring speech, "Confession of Faith." With luck, these would clinch the crucial votes. The final push was about to start when a campaign worker discovered a small line on each photograph that read "Moffett Studios—Chicago." Because Moffett held the copyright, unauthorized use of each photo could cost the campaign a dollar. The three million dollar price for distributing all the pamphlets greatly exceeded their resources. The campaign workers were in a tizzy. What to do?
>
> Not using the pamphlets would badly damage reelection prospects. Yet if they went ahead without Moffett's authorization and were found out, they'd be branded lawbreakers and would be liable for an unaffordable amount. Quickly, the campaign workers reached a consensus: they would have to negotiate with Moffett. It is not hard for us to imagine their queasy feeling as they tried to plot strategy. It must have seemed a hopelessly weak position: approaching a small photographic studio, in an obvious hurry, pamphlets already packed in railroad cars, a potential three million dollar price tag, and nowhere near that amount in the till.
>
> Dispirited, they approached George Perkins, noted financier and campaign manager. Perkins lost no time summoning his stenographer to dispatch the following cable: "We are planning to distribute many pamphlets with Roosevelt's picture on the cover. It will be great publicity for the studio whose photograph we use. How much will you pay us to use yours? Respond immediately." Shortly, he received this reply: "We've never done this before, but under the circumstances, we'd be pleased to offer you $250." Reportedly, Perkins accepted without asking for more.
>
> This story suggests a number of things about claiming value. First, many people readily assume that the bargaining range runs from the campaign paying nothing all the way up to three million dollars, or at least its total reserves. That the range could also include Moffett's paying

anything rarely occurs to people. This exemplifies how incorrect assumptions often fence us in.

This story helps explain the concepts of creating and claiming value. Perkins helped create value for Moffett through the advertising value that would accrue to his company by using its photograph of Roosevelt in a presidential campaign. Perkins claimed value by getting Moffett Studios to pay $250 dollars to have its photo selected.

However, there is a possible downside to this strategy! What if Moffett hadn't taken the bait? If Moffett had not responded, what would Perkins and the campaign team have done? Since they were in a hurry, with the pamphlets already packed in railway cars, they would have had to recontact Moffett and offer money to use the photograph. At that time, Moffett probably would have "smelled a rat," recognized that the campaign team was not bargaining in good faith, and so might have retaliated.

There is another possible downside to Perkin's strategy to hoodwink Moffett. If the press had found out, the potential bad publicity could have been devastating. Near the end of Fisher and Ury's (1981) book *Getting to Yes* is some excellent advice for negotiators. The book recommends that you conduct all negotiations as if your behavior during those negotiations will be a matter of public record. This is sage advice. It takes a long time to develop the reputation of being a principled and fair negotiator. It takes a very short time to destroy that reputation. Alway be aware that your reputation as a negotiator is one of your most important assets.

I now turn to some very interesting research on cooperative and aggressive negotiators, which sheds a great deal of light on the question of style and effectiveness, for your style of negotiating is inherently related to your ability to create and claim value.

### ▦ The Styles and Characteristics of Highly Effective Negotiators

One question frequently asked by participants in my training workshops is this: "Is there a difference in effectiveness between aggressive negotiators and cooperative negotiators?" I had found no research on the effectiveness of cooperative versus aggressive styles until I read an article titled "Style and Effectiveness in Negotiation," by Gerald R. Williams of the Faculty of Law at Brigham Young University. In his article, which describes a study of lawyers' behavior, Williams examines this crucial issue and concludes that "negotiating skills really do make a difference, and it is well worth our time to learn as much as we can about the patterns and characteristics of highly effective negotiators" (Williams, 1993, p. 154).

The main goal of this study was to identify the characteristics of highly effective negotiators. Those chosen for the study were all attorneys in the Denver, Colorado, metropolitan area. A questionnaire was mailed to a random sample. Each of these attorneys was asked to "think of an attorney against whom you have negotiated, who was so effective as a negotiator that you would hire that person to represent you if you were involved in a similar case in the future." They were also asked to think of an attorney they would rate as "average" and an attorney they would rate as "ineffective." All were then asked to rate each of these three types of attorneys—those rated highly effective, average, and ineffective—on 130 items relating to negotiator motivation, behavior, and traits.

The results of the study indicated that there are three distinct negotiating styles: "cooperative," "aggressive," and "no pattern." Each of these styles contains three subgroups rated on effectiveness of outcome. Williams labeled these three groups "effective," "average," and "ineffective." He concluded that our "effectiveness as a negotiator depends not on which approach we adopt but on how well we do within that particular strategy" (Williams, 1993, p. 158; see Figure 2.2).

Williams defines the "effective cooperatives" and the "effective aggressives" in terms of the objectives and the traits of each of these styles. Figure 2.3 summarizes these findings.

You need to understand the important distinctions between cooperative and aggressive styles if you are to negotiate effectively with people who use these styles. The differences between these styles are summarized below.

## Effective Cooperatives

> The highest-rated objective of negotiators who fell in the effective cooperative category is to "Conduct themselves ethically." The second-highest objective was "maximize" the settlement for their clients. . . . [Note that for the cooperatives] the word "maximize" is modified by item number three, "Get a fair settlement." [They] want to get a good outcome, but . . . [they] do not want to go beyond what would be fair to both sides. (Willams, 1993, p. 159)

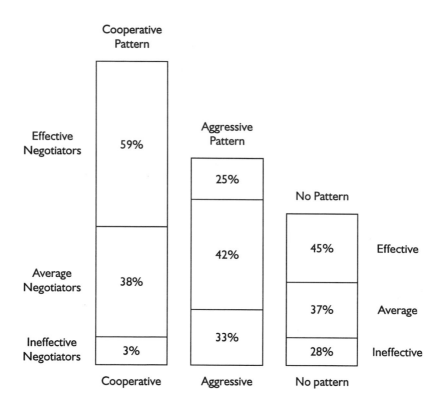

**Figure 2.2** Percentage of Attorneys in Each Category
SOURCE: Williams (1993). Reproduced by permission.

Cooperatives, then, are your quintessential "win-win" mutual-gains negotiators. Cooperatives want a good outcome for their client, but they also want the other side to be treated fairly. They would like both sides to feel good about the outcome and also about the process used to arrive at that outcome. Effective cooperatives excel at both creating and claiming value.

**Ineffective Cooperatives**

Ineffective cooperatives are too trustful, and this is their downfall in negotiations. Synonyms for "too trustful" include terms like "gullible," "naive," and "easily exploited." In describing the ineffective cooperatives, Williams (1993) adds that

| Cooperative Objectives | Aggressive Objectives |
|---|---|
| ▪ Conduct self ethically | ▪ Maximize settlement for client |
| ▪ Maximize settlement | ▪ Obtain profitable fee for self |
| ▪ Get a fair settlement | ▪ Outdo or outmaneuver opponent |

| Cooperative Traits | Aggressive Traits |
|---|---|
| ▪ Trustworthy<br>  Ethical<br>  Fair | ▪ Dominating<br>  Forceful<br>  Attacking |
| ▪ Courteous<br>  Personable<br>  Tactful<br>  Sincere | ▪ Plans timing and sequence of actions (strategy)<br>  Rigid<br>  Uncooperative |
| ▪ Fair minded | ▪ Carefully observes opponent |
| ▪ Realistic opening position | ▪ Unrealistic opening position |
| ▪ Does not use threats | ▪ Uses threats |
| ▪ Willing to share information | ▪ Reveals information gradually |
| ▪ Probes opponent's position | ▪ Willing to stretch the facts |

**Traits Shared by Both Types of Effective Negotiators**

- Prepared on the facts
- Prepared on the law
- Observes the customs and courtesies of the bar
- Takes satisfaction in using legal skills
- Effective trial attorney
- Self-controlled

**Figure 2.3**   Styles of Effective Cooperative and Aggressive Negotiators
SOURCE: From Williams (1993). Reproduced with permission.

in every videotape we have made that has a cooperative versus an aggressive negotiator, trustfulness is the fatal weakness of the ineffective cooperative.

[The second major factor that differentiated effective cooperatives from their ineffective counterparts was that the] ineffective cooperatives were too "gentle, obliging, patient, and forgiving. [And it seems they can never be] stirred up. . . . [N]o matter what happens, they are going to be polite and courteous, forgive you for what you do and try to get along with you." (p. 162)

It appears that not only are ineffective cooperatives not good at "claiming value" for themselves but, because they are so trusting and so forgiving, it encourages others to "claim value" against them. Ineffective cooperatives are your quintessential "muggables."

## Effective Aggressives

[For aggressives,] their highest-rated motive is to "Maximize the settlement for the client," then to "obtain a profitable fee" for themselves. But the most telling objective for effective aggressives is item number three: "Outdo or outmaneuver the opponent."

[Effective aggressives are] "win-lose negotiators; they want a clear winner and a clear loser . . . (And they want to be the winner).

Effective aggressives excel at claiming value. They tend to start with high demands and then accelerate if at all possible, assertively claiming as much value as they possibly can.

## Ineffective Aggressives

Williams found that ineffective aggressives were so demanding that they appeared to be obnoxious. More specifically, Williams (1993) stated,

One reason that ineffective aggressive negotiators are so obnoxious or irritating is that they make unreasonable opening demands or offers, even more extreme than their effective counterparts, and it is a pure bluff [since they tend to be unprepared on the facts]. With this in mind, it is easy to see why they are so irritating.

They use a take-it-or-leave-it strategy, [and tend to be] attacking, argumentative, quarrelsome, demanding, and aggressive.

[Third,] they are seen as rigid, egotistical, and headstrong.

[Fourth,] they are arrogant, disinterested in the needs of others, intolerant, and affirmatively hostile. (p. 163)

Williams postulates that 8% of negotiators make up the category "ineffective aggressives."

Ineffective aggressives excel at neither creating or claiming value. They start with such outrageous initial demands that the other party becomes so annoyed that the negotiation breaks off.

Williams rightly recommends that we "learn to recognize these patterns, to understand how they operate, to know when they are likely to be productive and when they are counterproductive, and most important, perhaps, how to deal with opponents in each of the patterns" (Williams, p. 161). One way to further examine these patterns is to look at what happens when the various types of negotiators negotiate in pairs. Consider the following combinations:

- Cooperative negotiator versus cooperative negotiator
- Cooperative negotiator versus aggressive negotiator
- Aggressive negotiator versus aggressive negotiator

It is possible to predict some general tendencies for each combination. A summary of Williams's findings appears below:

> The first combination, cooperative versus cooperative, is the most stable; if the problem can be solved, they will solve it.
>
> The third combination, aggressive versus aggressive, is intriguing. In a way, you might expect a brawl. But this often is not the case; although there is a higher risk of breakdown and the negotiation will take longer and consume more resources, the negotiators do speak the same language and do understand one another. They are also perfectly capable of cooperating with one another if they are convinced that is the better way to proceed.
>
> Now what about the second combination, cooperative versus aggressive? . . . [T]his combination is at the root of the majority of problems in negotiation, because these two negotiators do not speak the same language; they do not understand one another. They are operating on contrary assumptions.
>
> . . . [C]ooperative negotiators are trustworthy, ethical, and fair; they want a fair outcome; they adopt realistic positions; they avoid the use of threats; they disclose the facts early; and they value the prospect of agreement. In other words, cooperatives are problem solvers. How do they solve problems? On the merits; their instinct is to lay the facts out on the table. If I am a cooperative negotiator and I lay out my facts, and if you are cooperative, and you lay out your facts, then the two of us, as objective, fair-minded adults, can solve any problem. This is how cooperatives see their task. Against other cooperatives, this works very well. And since 65% of the negotiators in our study are basically cooperative, a cooperative will face another cooperative about 66% of the time.

But aggressive negotiators do not see themselves primarily as problem solvers, at least not in the same sense as cooperatives. They are warriors. Their strategy assumes the other side is an enemy to be attacked and defeated and their strategy is well adapted to that end. They are dominating, forceful, and attacking; they adopt more extreme positions; they use threats; they are reluctant to reveal information; and they seek a victory over the other side.

Which is the better strategy? Of course, we all prefer our own. Cooperatives feel their way is better; aggressives have no doubt it is their own. In my opinion they are both wrong, because when you need a problem solver or a healer nothing else will quite do, and when you really need a warrior, it is also true that nothing else will do. We cannot escape the reality that they are both legitimate and, in their time, indispensable.

The question is not: Which strategy should I invariable use? but rather: How can I develop sufficiently as a negotiator that I can appropriately invoke one or the other, depending on the requirements of the situation? I have come to believe that a fully developed negotiator should be capable of appropriately adopting either one in the proper circumstances. (pp. 164-165)

What does all of this research tell you about negotiating? First, you need to know your own primary style—cooperative or aggressive. Second, you need to examine how your style works with people who use a similar style. For example, if you are a cooperative negotiating with another cooperative, where does your style work for you, and where does it work against you? Or if you are an aggressive negotiating with another aggressive, where does your style work for you, and where does it work against you?

Perhaps the most interesting aspect of researching your own style's effectiveness will be the comparisons you make when negotiating with someone who uses a style different from your preferred one. For example, if you are an aggressive negotiating with a cooperative or a cooperative negotiating with an aggressive, you need to know where your style works and where you need to make changes in the way you negotiate.

By accurately diagnosing your own style first and then that of the person you are negotiating with, you are much more likely to negotiate effectively. You are also much more likely to make informed choices during the negotiation and therefore much more likely to negotiate outcomes that are favorable.

The next chapter contains information and exercises to help you diagnose your own negotiating style, and more important, the exercises will help you determine where your style works for you and where improvement is required.

# Assessing Your Current Negotiating Style

■ ■ ■ ■

The purpose of this chapter is to help you examine your current abilities as a negotiator and to formulate a list of ways to improve them. First, a seminal study is examined that looks at eight critical differences between effective senior managers and their average counterparts. You are then invited to rate your ability on each of these eight characteristics. The chapter concludes by looking at a strategy designed to help you assess how others see your current negotiating strengths and to highlight areas where improvement is desired.

## ■ Competency-Based Assessment

Successful organizations do not just happen—and they do not just stay successful. Great organizations are made up of individually successful managers who do the right things at the right time in the right circumstances. These managers are leaders who work with their people to create clear direction and vision, build effective teams, focus on customer needs, and practice sound business management.

—*Successful Manager's Handbook* (Davis et al., 1992, p. v)

A great deal of work has been done in the past 10 years on competency-based assessment, competency-based training, competency-based compensation, and competency-based succession planning. For example, I consulted a large retail firm that was in the position of retiring a large number of its senior managers in three years' time. Managers below the senior level were invited to apply for assessment for development for these positions. The application process involved intense examinations, the first of which was a competency-based evaluation titled "The Executive Success Profile." The profile is composed of 9 competencies, represented by 23 skills. These tests allow the participants to look at their relative strengths and weaknesses as seen by themselves, their boss, their peers, and their subordinates.

What this means is that successful organizations are choosing, promoting, and training their employees based on the best set of competencies and skills for each particular job in the company. A more specific description of the process can be found in a book titled *Competencies at Work* (Spencer & Spencer, 1993), which describes different sets of competencies needed for various types of jobs. The book even describes different types of competencies needed in the same type of job in different settings (e.g., a general manager for a research and development firm vs. a general manager in production). Although many of the competencies overlap, others are specific to one of the jobs or the other.

Of particular interest to negotiators is a study that examined the differences in skills and competencies between effective senior managers and their average counterparts. I describe this study in some detail because it tells you much of what you need to know to become more effective problem solvers and negotiators as well as more effective managers.

## ▦ Eight Essential Differences Between Effective Senior Managers and Their Average Counterparts

In general, there is a strong positive relationship between intelligence as measured by intelligence tests and performance in school. However, there is only a small positive relationship between intelligence test scores and competency on the job at the senior management level, accounting for an average of approximately 4% of the variance in on-the-job performance. One explanation for this low level of correspondence is that by the time people become successful enough to gain and maintain a job at this level their less intelligent counterparts have been weeded out.

The result is that 96% of individuals' success at this level can be attributed to competencies not measured by standard, academically oriented intelligence tests.

One question that researchers have been asking themselves is this: "Is there another method that could help us to define and measure these other factors?" Those who study "practical intelligence" or "competencies," as opposed to academic intelligence, believe there is. The key is to find methods to identify and measure this practical intelligence. For example, a study by Klemp and McClelland (cited in Sternberg & Wagner, 1986) examined the attributes that distinguished more successful senior managers from their less successful counterparts through a method called job competence assessment. The study used a sample of 132 senior managers drawn from six diverse types of organizations: general managers and division presidents from diversified *Fortune* 100 companies, executive directors from volunteer organizations, commanding officers from military hospitals, presidents and deans of universities, and senior executives from *Fortune* 100 financial service organizations.

The method of identifying the top performers involved both objective performance measures and nominations by others in the organization. An objective performance measure is obtained, for example, from figures on greatest financial growth. Examples of nomination by others are peer nominations or nomination by the CEO. For a person to be listed as a top performer, he or she had to be on all three lists. People who were not on any of the lists were listed as the average performers.

All senior managers were interviewed using the critical-incident method, which was designed to "uncover precise information on the actions and thoughts that make up competence in a given job" (p. 35). The results of the in-depth interviews showed that the "kinds of situations that top performers and average performers recall often differ significantly" (p. 36). Transcripts were made of all the interviews and read for themes that seemed to characterize the outstanding performers as a group, in contrast to the average performers.

The results of the study indicated that there are eight competencies that differentiate top senior managers from their average counterparts. These competencies fall into three categories: intellectual, influence, and self-confidence. Each of the eight competencies is next described within each of these three categories.

## Intellectual Competencies

Three intellectual competencies were identified in the study:

- *Planning/causal thinking.* This competency enables effective senior managers to "see distant consequences of today's activities and to design sound implementation strategies for their business or operations" (p. 38). The skills that make up this competency are anticipating problems or opportunities, identifying multiple implications of an action or event, accurately predicting outcomes of activities or events, taking action to avoid problems that are foreseen, identifying cause-and-effect relationships, anticipating future opportunities and requirements, stating implications of events and behavior, and stating thoughts in a causal sequence ("If X, then Y").
- *Diagnostic information seeking.* Specific skills that make up this competency are [pushing] for concrete information in ambiguous situations, [seeking] multiple sources to clarify a situation, and using high-yield questions to identify the specifics of a problem or situation. (p. 41)
- *Conceptualization/synthetic thinking.* The specific skills that make up this competency are understanding how different parts, needs, or functions of the organization fit together, [identifying] patterns, interpreting a series of events, [identifying] the most important issues in a complex situation, and using unusual analogies to understand or explain the essence of a situation. (p. 411)

Planning/causal thinking is essentially hypothesis generation because it involves seeing either the potential implications of events or the likely consequences of a situation based on what has usually happened in the past. By contrast, conceptualization/synthetic thinking is essentially theory building to account for consistent patterns in recurring events or for connections between seemingly unrelated pieces of information. Both are enhanced by diagnostic information seeking.

The competencies listed above are the ones usually taught in courses on management and leadership development. The second major skill set—the influencing skills—has not been taught in organizations until very recently.

## Influence Competencies

Four influence competencies were identified in the study:

- *Concern for influence.* This means alertness to the potentialities for influencing people. The indicators of this competency are essentially those used for scoring the need for power in the Thematic Apperception Test. Concern for influence appears in such statements as "When I walked into that meeting, I was trying to figure out how to persuade them to agree to my proposal." (pp. 40-41)
- *Directive influence.* This involves using one's personal authority or expert power to make sure that something gets done. [This] competency typically appears in a person's telling someone to do something, and it is particularly characteristic of first-line supervisors. (pp. 41-42)
- *Socialized power.* This is labeled in the study as a collaborative influence: "In management language, this is selling rather than telling: it is building relationships for the benefit of both parties; and it is operating effectively with groups in order to get cooperation." (p. 42)
- *Symbolic influence.* "It is indicated by a use of symbols to influence how people act in the organization. A senior manager with this competency can, by personal example or a statement of mission, create a sense of purpose for the whole organization, which engenders individuals' loyalty and commitment to it." (p. 42)

Effective managers have developed a negotiating and influencing style that works for them. Although they may have a preferred style, they are able to be flexible enough to choose from each of the four styles listed above or to select the correct combinations of styles to work effectively with a number of different types of people in a number of different types of situations.

## Self-Confidence: The Eighth Competency

According to Klemp and McClelland (in Sternberg & Wagner, 1986):

This important competency might well have been listed first, because we found it to be so prevalent among the outstanding senior managers. These people, although recognizing difficulties, never expressed any doubt that they would ultimately succeed. In the behavioral interviews, they displayed strong self-presentation skills and came across as very much in charge: they acted to make the interviewer feel comfortable, and they responded quickly and confidently to the request for key situations. By contrast, the average senior managers were more tentative, saying such things as, "To this day I don't know whether I made the right decision."

Moreover, the outstanding managers expressed self-confidence by being stimulated by crises and other problems, rather than distressed or overwhelmed by them. (p. 42)

### Interaction of the Competencies

These competencies work interactively. Therefore, training has to be developed that allows the participants to develop not only individual competencies but groups of functionally related competencies, as the following indicates:

For example, training programs in leadership and management skills, based on competency research, have been carried out in the U.S. Navy and have resulted in improved operational effectiveness. . . . Similarly, such indicators can be used [in selecting] the most promising candidates for senior management positions and, in performance appraisal, to help assess incumbents of those positions. (p. 48)

The model of training, negotiating, and influencing skills that was developed at the Harvard Project on Negotiation teaches competencies in the eight critical domains listed in the Klemp-McClelland research study. This training emphasizes learning the three intellectual competencies and the four influence competencies. Through becoming a better problem solver and improving one's negotiating skills, one's sense of self-confidence is built up.

The principle of modeling suggests that if you want to become more like the top people, no matter what their field, you need to develop a similar skill set.

■ ▓ ▒ ▓

### EXERCISE 3.1
#### Rating Your Competencies

You now have the opportunity to rate yourself on these eight critical competencies. The following competencies survey will help alert you to the areas in which your negotiating skills most need to be developed. To perform this test, rate yourself with an "X" on the following 10-point scales, which 1 is indicative of a low level of skill development and 10 is indicative of a high level of skill development:

### Rating Your Intellectual Competencies

1. *Planning/Causal Thinking:* "Planning/causal thinking is hypothesis generation, essentially. It involves seeing either the potential implication of events or the likely consequences of a situation based on what has usually happened in the past" (Klemp & McClelland, cited in Sternberg & Wagner, 1986, p. 40).

| I do not enjoy nor am I good at developing hypotheses and seeing the consequences for a situation based on what has happened in the past. | I enjoy and I am good at developing hypotheses and seeing the consequences for a situation based on past events. |
|---|---|

|   1   |   2   |   3   |   4   |   5   |   6   |   7   |   8   |   9   |   10   |

2. *Diagnostic Information Seeking:* Diagnostic information-seeking is pushing for concrete data in all sorts of ways, using a variety of sources to get as much information as possible to help with solving a particular problem. People who are good at diagnostic information-seeking are naturally curious and they ask questions to help them get the most data/information possible.

| I do not typically ask very many questions nor am I seen by others to engage in a great deal of diagnostic information seeking. | I typically ask a great many questions. Others see me engage in a great deal of diagnostic information seeking. |
|---|---|

|   1   |   2   |   3   |   4   |   5   |   6   |   7   |   8   |   9   |   10   |

3. *Conceptualization/Synthetic Thinking:* "[C]onceptualization/synthetic thinking is theory-building in order to account for consistent patterns in recurring events or for connections between seemingly unrelated pieces of information; it is enhanced by diagnostic information-seeking" (p. 40).

| I am not good at nor do I enjoy building theories from seemingly unrelated events or data. | I am good at and I enjoy building theories from seemingly unrelated or data. |

|  1    2    3    4    5    6    7    8    9    10  |

## Rating Your Influence Competencies

4. *Need or Desire to Influence Others:* The need for influence is "an alertness to the potentialities for influencing others." Concern for influence appears in such statements as 'When I walked into that meeting, I was trying to figure out how to persuade them to agree to my proposal. (p. 40)

| I do not have a strong need or desire to influence others. | I have a strong need or desire to influence others. |

|  1    2    3    4    5    6    7    8    9    10  |

5. *Directive Influence:* Directive influence measures the ability to "confront people directly when problems occur, [to tell] people to do things the way [you want] them done." (p. 41)

| I am not comfortable using my personal authority or expert power to make sure that something gets done. | I am comfortable using my personal authority or expert power to make sure that something gets done. |

|  1    2    3    4    5    6    7    8    9    10  |

6. *Collaborative Influence:* Collaborative influence measures the ability to operate "effectively with groups to influence outcomes and get cooperation, [to build] 'ownership' . . . among key subordinates by involving them in decision making." (p. 41)

I need improvement at building relationships for the good of both parties.

I am good at building relationships for the good of both parties.

| 1 | 2 | 3 | 4 | 5 | 6 | 7 | 8 | 9 | 10 |
|---|---|---|---|---|---|---|---|---|----|

7. *Symbolic Influence:* This last influence competency "is indicated by a use of symbols to influence how people act in the organization. A senior manager with this competency can, by personal example or a statement of mission, create a sense of purpose for the whole organization, which engenders individuals' loyalty and commitment to it." (p. 42)

I have difficulty leading others by enrolling them with a sense of mission.

I can easily lead others by enrolling them with a sense of mission.

| 1 | 2 | 3 | 4 | 5 | 6 | 7 | 8 | 9 | 10 |
|---|---|---|---|---|---|---|---|---|----|

**Rating Your Self-Confidence Competency**

8. *Self-Confidence:* Managers with strength in this competency, "although recognizing difficulties, never express any doubt that they will ultimately succeed. In behavioral interviews, they display strong self-presentation skills and come across as very much in charge. They act to make others feel comfortable, and they respond quickly and confidently to requests in key situations. By contrast, average senior managers are more tentative. Moreover, outstanding managers express self-confidence by being stimulated by crises and other problems rather than distressed or overwhelmed by them." (p. 42)

I have a low degree of self-confidence.

I have a high degree of self-confidence.

| 1 | 2 | 3 | 4 | 5 | 6 | 7 | 8 | 9 | 10 |
|---|---|---|---|---|---|---|---|---|----|

Based on your self-ratings of the above competencies, and knowing that competencies are made up of skill sets and that the whole is only as strong as the weakest link, which three skills do you most need to work on? The Skill Development Plan, which appears in Exercise 3.2, has been designed to help you in this important task.

▨ ▨ ▨ ▨

**EXERCISE 3.2**
**Skill Development Plan**

The three skills that I will develop further are:

1. _____

   Development Plan:

2. _____

   Development Plan:

3. _____

   Development Plan:

▨ ▨ ▨ ▨

## ▓ Feedback From People Who Know You Well and Will Tell You Honestly How They Perceive Your Negotiating Style

I was once asked to give a 90-minute presentation on time management. It was a challenging speaking engagement for two reasons. First, the audience consisted of adults and of children over age 9. I was worried that if I spoke to the parents I would lose the children and that if I spoke to the children I would lose the parents. To make matters worse, it was a murder mystery weekend, and the murder, complete with hearse and the Royal Canadian Mounted Police, took place just before my presentation was about to begin.

Luckily, I had planned to start with a very funny and well-done John Cleese film titled *The Unorganized Manager.* The film depicts the manager, Mr. Lewis, as being completely disorganized, which plays havoc with his management of time at work and at home. For example, the film shows Mr. Lewis forgetting his son's birthday and not having enough time to fix his son's new electric train. The audience loved the film and at least temporarily forgot about solving the murder mystery.

I knew that the next stage in my seminar was critical to its success: If I addressed the parents at this point, I would lose forever the participation of the children who were attending the workshop. Instead, I asked the children to rate Mr. Lewis on his time management ability as a father, by grading him with an A, B, C, D, or F. The children all responded, in loud unison, "F." I felt I was on a roll, so I picked one of the children and asked him how he would grade his father on time management. There was complete silence in the room. I was expecting him to say "A," "A−," maybe even "B−," but he said "C−." The father looked like he would kill the son, and then he looked like he would kill me.

I apologized to the father after the conference. He graciously accepted my apology, and then he said, "My son is 9 years old. In another nine years, he is going to leave our house. I don't want him to leave our house thinking that I am a 'C−' father."

This story illustrates two things: first, that salient feedback is very powerful and, second, that we live in a feedback-rich world. We just need to make more of an effort to obtain the feedback that is already there. It is important to have a sense of what you do well. Everyone needs and can benefit from positive feedback. Positive feedback also increases the likelihood that we will do the things that were positively reinforced or encouraged. We also need feedback on what we need to improve.

How can we use this technique to obtain more feedback about our own negotiating style? Simple. Ask three people who know you well to give you written feedback, using the form in Exercise 3.3. The form asks them to list three things that you do well as a negotiator and to list three targets for improvement.

The exercise works best when you choose for your respondents insightful people who will be honest with you and will give you unbiased feedback. For instance, if you are on your way to the divorce court with your ex-spouse, this is probably not the right person or the right time to ask for unbiased feedback.

The exercise works well only if the feedback is specific. Once the forms are filled out and returned to you, look at the repetitive feedback you received. Where there are inconsistencies in the comments, it may be that the respondents see you differently because you behave differently in different relationships, or it may be that the respondents are telling you more about themselves than about you.

■ ■ ■ ■

## EXERCISE 3.3
### Negotiation Feedback Form

List three things that you like about _____'s negotiating style. Please be as specific as possible. Simply saying "John is a good communicator" is not specific enough. It should be so specific that John will know exactly what he should do more of in the future. For example, a specific comment would be "John is very good at coming up with creative solutions. He always invents at least three options to be considered at every negotiation."

THANK YOU.

1.

2.

3. List three specific targets for improving _____'s negotiating style:

   a.

   b.

   c.

■ ■ ■ ■

In this chapter, you have evaluated your negotiation/conflict management style using two instruments: Rating the Eight Competencies and the Negotiation Feedback Form. In Chapter 2, you rated your effectiveness in the exercise "Creating and Claiming Value." Now is the time to integrate these findings.

■ ■ ■ ■

### EXERCISE 3.4
### Integrated Assessment

1. What are three areas these instruments agree on in relation to your negotiation strengths?

   a.

   b.

   c.

2. What are three areas these instruments agree on for improvement in your negotiation style?

   a.

   b.

   c.

3. Were there any questions raised about your negotiation style that need further clarification, understanding, and/or more information/data before you can improve them?

■ ■ ■ ■

# Principles and Techniques for Creating and Claiming Value

■ ■ ■ ■

This chapter explains the 10 essential differences between effective negotiators and their less effective counterparts. The chapter then introduces you to the critical importance of preparation and muscle level in regard to how much power you need to bring to the negotiating table. Also examined are several techniques to get stalled negotiations back on track. The chapter then examines the strategic role of "frames" in helping you become more persuasive and the critical role of "precedent setting" in the negotiation process.

## ■ 10 Differences Between Effective Negotiators and Their Less Effective Counterparts

### 1. The Power of Preparation

As a general rule, the most successful people in the world are those who have the best information.

*—Disraeli*

There are three essential factors in every negotiation: preparation, preparation, and preparation. In fact, William Ury of the Harvard Program on Negotiation states that 50% of the time you spend on a negotiation should be spent in preparation, the first stage of which involves preparation on the facts and on the assumptions underlying the negotiation.

### Preparation on Facts and Assumptions

You are not ready to negotiate until you have all the essential information. Before you start the negotiations, you have to ask yourself "Do I have all the facts?" and "Am I starting this negotiation on an invalid assumption?" The following story illustrates these points.

My wife and I bought a set of flats (apartments) as our first home. We lived upstairs, and our tenants lived downstairs. After having lived there for over a year and after receiving some very good information on energy conservation, we decided that the temperature of the hot water could easily be lowered by several degrees. I went into the basement and turned the hot water heater thermostat down by 5°.

Over the next several days, we noticed that the hot water seemed hotter than ever. I returned to the basement and lowered the thermostat by several more degrees. The next day, we noticed that the hot water seemed hotter still.

I again returned to the basement and lowered the thermostat by 10°. The next day, the hot water was scaldingly hot. I returned to the basement and looked carefully at the controls. The temperature was set at 55° F, yet the hot water was uncomfortably hot. I checked the connection from the hot water tank to the oil tank, and indeed, my hot water tank was hooked up to my fuel tank. Where was the problem?

As you may have guessed, I assumed that my hot water tank was hooked up to our flat. It wasn't. A plumber, at some time in the past, had made a serious mistake. He connected our hot water tank to our tenants' flat and, conversely, connected their hot water tank to our flat. Every time I turned the thermostat down, they had experienced a lowering of their hot water temperature. They subsequently turned their thermostat up, and the temperature of the hot water in our flat increased.

▦ ▦ ▦ ▦

**EXERCISE 4.1**
**Improving Fact Finding**

1. In the space below, briefly describe a situation in which not having all the facts caused you to be a less effective negotiator than you could have been.

2. What do you have to do to better gather all the necessary facts in the future?

▦ ▦ ▦ ▦

Beside your preparation on the facts, you must make sure that you are not proceeding under unwarranted assumptions. Much of your effectiveness as a negotiator involves carefully looking at your assumptions, as the following incident suggests. The incident took place at the local sports center. I had just finished a nice, long, hot shower after working out. After shaving, I turned to dry my hands under the electric dryer. Suddenly I felt a tremendous pain, let out a pained "ouch!" and turned around to find a 180-pound young man wearing steel-tipped Kodiak boots—who had just stepped on my toes. I was just about to say "Why don't you look where you are going!" when I noticed that the young man was blind. I felt two inches tall.

Good negotiators verify their assumptions. Excellent negotiators look at their assumptions about their assumptions. The best negotiators verify their assumptions about their assumptions about their assumptions. As a famous marriage therapist states, "It's not who decides that causes problems in a marriage, it's who decides, who decides, who decides." Good negotiation is also good assumption management. Keeping a log of your assumptions, both the ones that work and the ones that don't, will help you to increase your negotiation effectiveness.

The above does not mean that you can ever be perfectly prepared. Often, you need to get additional information and/or further verify or clarify the information that you do have. Once you have completed your preparation on the facts and the assumptions underlying the negotiation, you need to prepare your opening statement. A large percentage of the outcome of the negotiation depends on a well-prepared opening.

## The Importance of an Opening Statement Based on Jointly Determined Principles

Consider the following example from labor/management negotiations. The North American telephone industry has changed drastically with deregulation. In place of regional monopolies, many excellent firms are fiercely battling it out in the marketplace. There are really only two major ways to compete—price and service. To survive, these companies have to be excellent at both.

One such regional telephone company's market share was being threatened by new competitors for its long-distance services. As a consequence, the company was undergoing drastic changes in the way it conducted its business both externally and internally. This particular negotiation to look at concerned a new selection method in hiring telephone customer service representatives. The company's position was that to remain competitive it had to hire people who were not only very comfortable talking on the telephone but also had the potential to become excellent service providers and company representatives.

In the past, the selection procedure for these positions was done using verbal, face-to-face, structured interviews. The phone company was in the process of changing to a competence-based selection approach whereby the interviewing process would begin with "a customer" calling for service over "the telephone." The company felt that the telephone simulation was the best way to assess for the skills necessary for actual on-the-job performance. Paul, who was the manager in charge of the telephone company's negotiation with the union, had developed the company's case based on its need to become more efficient and more effective.

The union's position was that the new procedure was unfair. The union felt that by doing telephone simulations first, many of the applicants would experience stress, which would negatively affect their performance. Therefore, some qualified applicants would not be selected for the positions. The negotiation was turning into a classic management/union standoff.

I worked with Paul to improve the likelihood of his getting a workable agreement with the union. The first thing I said to him was that it was important, early in the negotiation, to work out an agreement with the union based on principle. Therefore, the first thing we did was to work on his opening statement. Paul's original opening statement concerned the company's need for efficiency and effectiveness. However, he implied that fairness—the union's concern—was not as important as his concerns for "effectiveness" and "efficiency." To have the most effective impact, he needed to state both his and the union's concerns as joint concerns, because in an era of increased competition it is also in the union's best interests that the company do well or there will be fewer jobs to protect.

We then talked about the "Golden And." Bruce Patton of the Harvard Program on Negotiation speaks eloquently about the need to recognize the complexity of many problems before they can be resolved. The "Golden And" recognizes the complexity of problems by recognizing the legitimacy of what are or what appear to be conflicting interests. As Bruce says, "the word 'but,' stated or implied, is the great eraser." The statement before the word "but" is seen as much less important than the statement following it. For example, a husband tells his wife that she cooked an excellent meal, *but* the roast was slightly overdone. Nine times out of 10, all his wife will hear is that the roast was overdone. In contrast to using the word "but," using the word "and" opens up possibilities for creative problem solving.

The goal to help both the company and the union do well is a superordinate one. Superordinate goals are important because they are more inclusive than each group's individual goals. From doing this exercise, Paul realized he had to change his opening statement. He started the subsequent meeting in the following manner:

> In light of the increased competition that the phone company is facing, it is important for the company and for the union that the company become as effective and as efficient as possible because it is only through being effective and efficient that we can support our jobs. And it is also important

that we select people for jobs in this company in a manner that is and appears to be fair. Can we discuss options that will meet our mutual concerns for effectiveness, efficiency, and fairness?

It would be very difficult for anyone to disagree with the above statement. In fact, it allowed management and the union to reach their first agreement. Now all that remained was to work out details that would help them do just that. In the next step, the union and management generated options that would meet the stated criteria of being effective, efficient, and fair. Among the options generated were these:

- Allowing the applicants two practice simulations on the phone before their actual assessment
- Conducting short verbal interviews before the simulations to help the applicants understand the process
- Instituting the new system for a three-month trial run and then assessing the procedure for fairness by both management and union representatives
- Demonstrating a new assessment method to the union and work to overcome their concerns
- Developing a new assessment method that would be more fair to the applicants than the previous system, as there would be less room for interview bias.

This story also illustrates the power of reaching agreements "in principle" early in the negotiation. Once this preliminary agreement is reached, it can be used effectively to guide subsequent agreements and help resolve "the details" that must be agreed to later in the negotiation. Good opening statements emphasize the following:

- Win/win and/or mutual benefit
- Core values and/or principles
- Identification of superordinate goals
- Agreement on the benefits of negotiating and/or costs of not negotiating

Good opening statements are the foundation. Agreements are then built on previous agreements until a good outcome is in place that helps resolve the conflict.

■ ■ ■ ■

**EXERCISE 4.2**
**Developing Opening Statements**

Using the preceding as a model, write an effective opening statement for a negotiation you are in now or are about to enter. Critique your opening statement on mutual benefits, core values or principles, use of superordinate goal(s), benefits to negotiating, and/or the cost of not negotiating. Then ask several good negotiators to critique your opening statements from time to time.

■ ■ ■ ■

## 2. The Power of Asking Questions

■   Questions Educate

One of the most important competencies listed in *Competencies at Work* (Spencer & Spencer, 1993) is information seeking. The best informed people usually make the best decisions. One of the things true of well-informed people is that they are good at "information seeking." People who are good information seekers get better information sooner and with more ease. One of the trademarks of good information seekers is their ability to ask questions.

Most people go into a negotiation assuming that they have all the answers and all the facts. It is their job, therefore, to educate the other party in the negotiation. Roger Fisher of the Harvard Program on Negotiation states that you are better off making the opposite assumption: that there is an important piece of information you do not have but by asking the right question in the right way at the right time that piece of information will help you unlock the solution to the negotiation.

The following example illustrates the difference between high-yield and low-yield questions. Please note that this difference is not the same as the difference between open-ended and closed questions. High-yield questions are distinguishable by the amount of useful information you receive from asking the question. Thus, high-yield questions can be both open ended and closed. Using closed-ended questions can be very valuable because they quickly tell you whether or not to pursue an area with further questioning. Also, note that high-yield questions are emotionally neutral, do not make the other party feel defensive, or push for a "politically correct" answer but, rather, invite the other party to think about and explore his or her feelings, thoughts, beliefs, and values.

My example involves a friend of mine named Pat, who told me that he was perplexed about the negative reaction he was having about his daughter's request to change from figure skating to hockey. I asked him some low-yield questions:

> Why are you so uncomfortable with your daughter playing hockey? After all, your son plays hockey.
> Don't you think that you're being a bit unfair to your daughter?
> Aren't you being a bit chauvinistic?

Then I asked some high-yield questions:

> Are there other girls playing hockey in your area?
> Have you asked your daughter what she likes about playing hockey?
> Have you considered a course in "power skating" for hockey so she can test her desire to play hockey?
> If you had a son as a second child, would you want him to play hockey?
> Are you concerned about your daughter's safety?

It turned out that in our conversation the high-yield question about safety was the most powerful. Pat told me that his daughter was seriously injured as an infant, and he was concerned about her being reinjured if she were to play hockey. He was also concerned that the real reason why she wanted to play hockey was because her older brother did. Pat then said that enrolling his daughter in "power skating" might give both of them the additional information they needed to make a "wise" decision about her playing hockey.

### EXERCISE 4.3
### Asking High-Yield Questions

Observe several of the best negotiators you know. Watch how they use high-yield questions. What have you learned that will increase your effectiveness in asking high-yield questions? In the space below, write down what you have learned and then prepare several high-yield questions for your next negotiation.

■ ■ ■ ■

When asking "why?" does not work, try presenting your proposal and ask "why not?" Generally speaking, people who withhold information are feeling critical. By asking "why not?" they then criticize your proposal and, in doing so, are telling you about their interests and priorities.

■    The Value of Pausing

Another of the major differences between effective negotiators and their less effective counterparts is the ability to pause. In teaching and observing negotiations, I have seen people ask incredibly good information-seeking questions but then not wait long enough to get an answer or answer the question themselves. Effective negotiators have learned how to be comfortable with silence. They have mastered the four-second pause: "one thousand, two thousand, three thousand, four thousand." Pausing makes it much more likely that you will hear the information you need to negotiate effectively.

■ ■ ■ ■

**EXERCISE 4.4**
**Effective Pausing**

Observe the people you are negotiating with. Who pauses effectively? Who does not? What effect does pausing and not pausing have? Next, observe yourself negotiating. When do you pause effectively? When don't you?

■ ■ ■ ■

### 3. The Power of Awareness of Choice Points

Choice points are critically important points in a negotiation that are pivotal to its outcome. If you make the right decision at a choice point, the negotiation will move forward toward resolution. If you make the wrong decision, the negotiation will move toward a break-off, stalemate, or escalation.

The following story from *When Families Fight* (Rubin & Rubin, 1989) illustrates the importance of choice points and options. In the story, both father and son make choices that lead toward escalation of the fight between them. As you read the story for the first time, put yourself in the role of the father and underline his choice points. Then read the story a second time and, using a double line or a different-colored pen or pencil, underline the choice points for the son.

## The Escalation of a Fight

It started out as not much of a fight at all. Joe, 16, had borrowed Dad's car for the night and was supposed to fill up the tank, but did not. The next morning, Dad was late for work because he had to wait in line for gasoline in the middle of rush-hour traffic. That evening, Dad let Joe know how much inconvenience his forgetfulness had caused. Joe apologized, but in that moderate and off-hand adolescent way—while looking over his shoulder at the Celtics-Knicks game on TV.

That was when things started to heat up. Miffed at what he saw as Joe's lack of real concern, Dad remarked again on Joe's inconsiderate and irresponsible behavior. Joe's response, grunted between bites of [microwave] pizza and slurps of Coke, was found wanting. Now, a real apology was demanded. Since it was not quickly forthcoming, Dad started to bring out the records of previous behavior that reinforced the image of an irresponsible and inconsiderate kid. Clothes strewn about, lawns left uncut, drinking all of the orange juice and putting the empty container back in the fridge. The list continued.

After a few minutes of this, Joe decided that he had had enough. He exploded. "Who are you to tell me what to do? I don't see you doing much around here. When was the last time you did the dishes? As far as you're concerned, I don't do anything right. All you do is complain about me and everyone else in the family. You don't really care how other people in the family feel, do you?"

"And you don't care about anyone but yourself, Mister," came the response. "You can forget about using the car again, too."

Now Mom enters into the conversation! "He's had exams, a lot of pressure, we all make mistakes," she says to her husband. "Gee, give him a break, honey."

"Why don't you butt out, okay? I had an important meeting, and I missed it because of this self-centered, arrogant [son of yours] who can't think about anybody but himself. Why don't you stay out of this? You always spoil him and defend him, which is why he's so undisciplined, anyway!"

"I will not have you speaking to me in that tone of voice," says Mom. "When you think you can be civil again, let me know!" With that, she leaves the room, followed by Joe's kid sister, and shortly by Joe. There sits Dad, alone, wondering what happened. "Why did I become so angry? What went wrong?"

How negotiations begin is critically important. A rough rule of thumb is that 90% of the outcome of all negotiations depends on how they start. So let's go back to the beginning. If you were negotiating in this case, as the father, what would you do about the television? Please list at least four options in the space below. (A good rule of thumb is that you are not ready to negotiate unless you have at least four options at your disposal.)

1.

2.

3.

4.

When role-playing this situation in my workshops, most people's first reaction is to turn off the television set. However, if you list your options first, you are much more likely to choose the best option for that particular situation at that particular time. Among your options here are the following:

- Turn off the television set.
- Talk to Joe during a commercial break.

- Talk to Joe after the hockey game.
- Talk to Joe while the game is on.
- Tell Joe you want to speak to him about the car after the game.
- Talk to him about the car now; record the game on the VCR.


Before you consider which option you want to choose, consider the "prize" (the desired outcome from the negotiation). On one level, the prize is an apology from Joe. On another level, the prize is having Joe fill up the gas tank when he uses Dad's car. On a deeper level still, the prize is the opportunity to teach his son about adult responsibility. Psychologists call this type of critical point a "teachable moment." Teachable moments don't come all that often. As a professional negotiator, you must develop your awareness of being at a teachable moment.

For example, when my son Andrew was 4-and-a-half years old, we were driving down a street near our house when I noticed that the traffic had slowed and that, kitty-corner to where we were turning, a pedestrian was lying on the sidewalk after having been hit by a car. I went for my first reaction, which was to turn the corner quickly so Andrew would not see the accident. Several minutes later, I realized what I had done. This had been a teachable moment, the perfect opportunity to teach Andrew about the consequences of not practicing traffic safety—and I had not seen it at the time. I did, however, acknowledge my increased awareness, which meant that I would be more likely to effectively use the teachable moment next time.

Teachable moments are one subcategory of choice points. As a negotiator, you must increase your awareness that you are at a choice point before you can act differently. One of the ways to act differently at that moment is to consider what the prize (desired outcome) is and which of the options at your disposal are most congruent with working toward that prize.

Returning to our negotiation with Joe, depending on the prize sought you would select from the options above very differently:


- The first option, turning off the television, is likely to make Joe angry, which would take away from his complete attention. Teaching about "adult responsibility" requires full attention.
- Talking to Joe after the game would work for Joe, but it might not help to alleviate any of Dad's frustration.

- Talking to Joe during a break does not leave enough time to fully discuss the problem.
- Recording the game on the VCR may not allow Joe to fully concentrate on solving the problem or discuss the issue of adult responsibility.
- Telling Joe that there was a problem regarding gas in the car and reaching an agreement to talk after the game may be the optimal strategy in this case.

By listing and considering all of your options, you are more likely to consider the best option in each particular issue.

In summary, choice points are those critical times in any negotiation when informed decisions are likely to lead to a productive resolution of the problem. Good negotiators are much more likely to be aware that they are at choice points and thus make informed vigilant decisions. Uninformed choices are likely to lead to nonvigilant or hypervigilant decisions, which can result in breaking off the negotiations, a stalemate, or escalation of the problem.

## 4. The Power of Identifying Interests

Identifying interests is one of the most important skills that good negotiators have developed. This section examines the power of identifying interests to help resolve a difficult situation. You are then invited to apply these same skills to help better resolve a negotiation that you are currently in or are preparing for. The last part of this section looks at the power of identifying additional interests, which at first may seem unrelated to the problem, to expand the pie to create solutions that would otherwise not be possible.

### Identifying Interests

I have been teaching and coaching others in how to be more effective negotiators for the past 12 years. During this time, I have developed several very good case studies and also have used those developed at the Harvard Program on Negotiation to help teach negotiating skills. Therefore, I have been able to watch literally thousands of people negotiate the same cases. I have observed that one of the areas that most clearly differentiates good negotiators from poor ones, and good outcomes from poor ones, is the ability to identify interests—both yours and those of the other party (parties) with whom you are negotiating. My own observations and that of my colleagues who teach negotiation skills is that most people think they are better at identifying interests than they really are. Both the lack of awareness that their skills are not as good as they think they are and an actual lack of skills keep most people from being as effective when negotiating as they would like to be. One of the best ways to learn these skills of identifying interests is by studying a good example and then systematically applying these skills in your own negotiations.

Let's look at a situation where the power of identifying interests helps a newly married couple resolve a potentially difficult problem. In this example, Eric and Gail have been married for six months, and this is the second marriage for both. They each hold high-pressure middle-management positions and have been unable to schedule time to take their honeymoon until now. They are looking forward to a memorable honeymoon and have planned to drive to Quebec City, which is one of North America's most romantic cities. Because this is the off-season, they were able to book their hotel at an excellent rate. However, to get the heavily discounted rate their reservations are nonrefundable.

Gail is a project manager in the IT (information technology) department of a large multinational company. She is working on a project that involves the conversion from an old accounting/database management program to a new state-of-the-art one. Hers is the last of the company's branch operations to undergo the conversion. Let us further assume that the conversion to the new program must be completed for startup next Monday which is March 17, 1997, and today is Tuesday, March 11. This leaves four working days to complete the upgrade.

Gail has an excellent team of six people, including herself, in her department. So far, they are on target for finishing the project. Unfortunately, when Gail arrived at work this morning, there were messages from three of her team members, all of whom had come down with a severe case of this year's worst flu. They are all running high temperatures, and it is very doubtful that they will be able to return to work any time soon. By noon, another member of her department goes home sick. Getting all the work done by Friday so that she can leave on her honeymoon on Saturday is looking impossible.

Gail approaches her supervisor, Peter, and tells him about her concerns in getting the conversion finished in time. Peter tells Gail, in no uncertain terms, that failure is not an option. The head office expects that the conversion

| Eric's Interests | Gail's Interests |
|---|---|
| ▓ Have a Memorable Honeymoon | ▓ Have a Memorable Honeymoon |
| ▓ Support Gail's Career | ▓ Successfully Complete the Project |
| ▓ Not Lose Their Nonrefundable Deposit on Their Honeymoon Vacation | ▓ Have a Good Chance at the Promotion |
| ▓ Have A Good Marriage | ▓ Have A Good Marriage |
| ▓ Have His Feelings Respected | ▓ Have Her Feelings Respected |
| ▓ Develop a Wise Solution to This Problem | ▓ To Develop a Wise Solution to This Problem |
| ▓ Increase Their Disposable Income | ▓ Increase Their Disposable Income |
| ▓ Develop a Solution That Will Be a Model for Resolving Future Problems | ▓ Develop a Solution That Will Be a Model for Resolving Future Problems |

**Figure 4.1**    Turning Issues Into Interest

will be finished and working by Monday so that the head office's IT department can finish its year-end reports on time for the board meeting. Peter then tries to sweeten the blow by telling Gail that a position in upper middle management is opening up some time during the year and that her finishing the project will greatly increase her chances of obtaining that position, one that Gail has had her eyes on for years. But what about the honeymoon? Eric has been talking about nothing else. To make matters worse, Eric's first wife was a workaholic, so even the idea of talking to Eric about changing their honeymoon could be a very sensitive topic for him.

Under most circumstances, this could lead to a difficult conflict between Eric and Gail. Let's see how they used interest-based negotiation to resolve their problem by using the Turning Issues Into Interests worksheet (Figure 4.1).

By writing down and looking at their shared and differing interests, Gail and Eric are more likely to separate the people from the problem and to focus on the problem. They are also much more likely to see all the elements of the problem and to see which interests they have in common. All of this will make solving the problem that much easier. Also, this couple clearly saw the importance of resolving this problem with a wise solution because it will set a precedent for how any future problems/disputes are settled.

▓    Developing Options to Satisfy Interests

The next step is to brainstorm options that satisfy as many interests as possible. Please remember that the basic rule of brainstorming is that during

- Postpone the honeymoon completely.
- See if the hotel will allow a change of dates and if Gail's company will pay the difference in the cost of their hotel reservations if that proves necessary.
- See if there are other people either within or outside Gail's company who can help her get the project completed on time.
- Process the data from Gail's branch operation at another site and complete the upgrade after Gail returns from her honeymoon.
- Eric could drive up to Quebec City and visit one of his best friends in Montreal, and Gail can fly up after she completes the conversion.

**Figure 4.2**   Possible Options for Gail and Eric

the inventing-of-options phase *no* criticism is allowed. In other words, evaluating the options does not take place during the brainstorming phase. The reason for this is that you don't want to inhibit the creative process. Even the most far-fetched idea may contain a part of the ideal solution, or it may spark another idea that either is or is close to an ideal solution. Some possible options from the case of Gail and Eric are presented in Figure 4.2.

■ ■ ■ ■

### EXERCISE 4.5
### Turning Issues Into Interests

For the purpose of this exercise, please use the worksheet below to identify all the interests for all parties in a negotiation you are currently in or use it to help you prepare for an upcoming negotiation. (Extra copies of this worksheet can be made from the one in Appendix B.)

### TURNING ISSUES INTO INTERESTS

Issues for Party #1                              Issues for Party #2

| Interests for Party #1 | Interests for Party #2 |
|---|---|
| 1. | 1. |
| 2. | 2. |
| 3. | 3. |
| 4. | 4. |
| 5. | 5. |
| 6. | 6. |
| 7. | 7. |
| 8. | 8. |
| 9. | 9. |
| 10. | 10. |

▓ ▓ ▓ ▓

## ▓ The Power of Identifying Additional Interests

There are many instances where resolving a problem appears to be impossible. However, if you listen carefully enough and if you look for underlying or hidden interests, these underlying or hidden interests are often the "key" to help you unlock the negotiation as the following example points out.

As parents, my wife and I pride ourselves on not letting Nintendo® into our home, as we feel that it has little educational value. However, if the truth be known, we have almost identical games on our home computer. Our 7-year-old son Andrew particularly loved to play one of them, called "Captain Z." As with all arcade games, the player has to master succeedingly more difficult levels in order to win. Although we did not like the game, we did admire Andrew's perseverance in trying to master it.

Finally, one night Andrew finished "Captain Z." Instead of being delighted, he was crestfallen. In the last scene of the game, Captain Z disappears down a hole, and a moment later a bulletin appears on the screen announcing that the adventure continues on disks 2 and 3, along with instructions on how to order them. Andrew immediately asked us to order these.

My wife was adamant that we would not buy any more of this type of game. I felt the same way but didn't think it was fair to Andrew to be so disappointed after working so hard.

I thought about it for a day and couldn't come up with any viable solutions until I considered other interests that my wife and I had. One of these was getting Andrew to use the word processor for children that I had installed on the computer. The word processor allows the child to type a story, and then a voice synthesizer in the program reads the story back to the child. There was only one problem: Andrew did not like to use it.

It occurred to me that we could probably make a deal with our son to meet his interests and ours. I suggested to him that we would order disks 2 and 3 of "Captain Z" if he would write 10 stories on his word processor, after which I would install the next episode of "Captain Z." Andrew responded by writing two stories a day so that he could continue with "Captain Z" by the end of the week.

The outcome of this story is that everyone's interests were met. Andrew got to continue playing his favorite game, and we got what we wanted, for Andrew wrote enough stories on the word processor that he began to appreciate both it and his ability as a writer.

My experience and that of others I have talked with who teach negotiation skills have led me to believe that identifying interests is not only one of the most important skills any negotiator can possess but also something most people think they do better than they actually do. In other words, not adequately identifying their interests and not adequately preparing a BATNA (Best Alternative to a Negotiates Agreement) (Fisher & Ury, 1981) are the two factors that keep most negotiators from being as effective as they could or they should. The following form has been designed to help make sure that you have thoroughly identified both parties' interests both before and during the negotiating process.

▨ ▨ ▨ ▨

## EXERCISE 4.6
### Identifying Additional and Hidden Interests

Think of three negotiations where you, or the party you were negotiating with, or another person looked for and discovered additional interests that made it possible to reach an agreement.

1.

2.

3.

What have you learned from this exercise that will make it more likely that you will discover and add additional interests in your future negotiations?

▓ ▓ ▓ ▓

## 5. The Power of Muscle Level

"Muscle level" is the amount of power or force you use in a negotiation. In exercising your power during a negotiation, there are two mistakes you can make: using too much too soon and using too little too late.

Muscle Level can be illustrated by an example from the medical profession, called "the principle of least intrusion."

Suppose you are suffering from mild stomach pain from gastritis (a condition resulting from too much acid in the stomach) and you decide to visit your physician. At Muscle Level 1, your physician would prescribe a bland diet—no caffeine, no chocolate, no alcohol, no fried food, and no spicy foods.

If your condition did not clear up, or if it worsened, your physician would move on to Muscle Level 2. At this stage, your doctor would probably prescribe an antacid. In addition to the bland diet, you would be asked to take a dose of antacid after every meal and before bedtime.

If your condition still did not clear up, or if it worsened, your physician would move on to Muscle Level 3. At this level, your doctor would probably prescribe a medication that inhibits the stomach from producing acid.

If your condition still did not clear up, or if you developed further problems, such as bleeding ulcers, your doctor would apply Muscle Level 4, perhaps by hospitalizing you for bed rest. The medication that inhibits the stomach from producing acid would be delivered intravenously to ensure a constant and steady supply.

If your condition still did not clear up, or if it worsened to the point where you could die of bleeding ulcers, your physician would move to

Muscle Level 5 and likely schedule you for surgery to cut the vagus nerve, which is the nerve that stimulates the stomach to produce acid.

If the first time you visited your physician with minor stomach pains you had been scheduled for surgery you would most likely have gotten a second opinion because the doctor had escalated too soon and too fast. How can you prevent yourself from doing the same thing during a negotiation? You can take a break and think about which of the muscle levels can be applied effectively to your negotiation by writing down what you would do at Muscle Levels 1, 2, 3, and so on. Doing this will make it much less likely that you will allow yourself to unconsciously escalate too quickly.

The appropriate use of a muscle level is described as follows:

- Muscle Level 1 is a polite request: "I'd like you to let us know when you can't come to a steering committee meeting."

- Muscle Level 2 is a request that is stronger in word choice, voice characteristics, and body language: "When you don't let us know that you're going to miss a meeting, we sometimes end up meeting without a quorum, which is useless. I need to know when you can't make a meeting."

- Muscle Level 3 is a statement of consequences if the behavior doesn't change: "If you can't let us know when you'll miss a meeting, we will have to ask you to resign from the committee."

- Muscle Level 4 is the application of the consequences stated in Level 3: "Since you have not been keeping us informed about your attendance, I will have to ask you to leave the committee."

—*Drury* (1984, pp. 49-50)

Escalating too soon and too fast also can be quite costly, as the following story illustrates. Several years ago, I was asked to teach a week-long course in Africa on negotiating. I was to work closely with a local trainer for three weeks prior to teaching the course to the students, so that the skills for teaching the course could be passed on after I returned to North America. The local trainer was responsible for helping make the course material culturally relevant to his country. Unfortunately, the person assigned to this job put very little effort into learning the material. I was working morning, afternoon, and evening, and he was goofing off. By the second week, I had had it. I confronted him at Muscle Level 3 and ended up damaging our working relationship. It turned out that he was very well connected politically, and

I had significantly reduced the chances of my being invited back to that country for additional work.

Please note: I am not saying that I should not have confronted him. I should have. But whereas at Muscle Level 2 I might have had a chance of resolving our difference of opinion regarding a more equitable sharing of the work load, at Muscle Level 3 I resolved nothing and lessened the chance of resolving our differences. I learned my lesson. When angry, write down your plan (action/response) for each muscle level. This will make it much more likely that you will respond with the appropriate amount of power.

One way to help you become more familiar with this important tool and to increase your effectiveness as a negotiator is to complete the following exercise.

■ ■ ■ ■

## EXERCISE 4.7
### Using the Appropriate Muscle Level

1. Note a recent situation in which you escalated your muscle level too soon.

2. What were the negative consequences of escalating too quickly?

3. What would you do differently next time?

■ ■ ■ ■

Now let's look at an example of not using enough muscle soon enough. A client came to see me for help with his marriage. The presenting problem was that he and his wife were arguing more frequently. I suggested marital counseling, but his wife decided that she would not attend. We explored his options, and it became obvious that he was very conflicted about staying in the relationship. They had no children, and the problems had been fairly severe in nature for the past four years.

I helped this man explore his options. Finally, he decided he couldn't take it any longer and told his wife he wanted a trial separation and that he would begin looking for a furnished apartment. He again asked her if she would consider marriage counseling, and she said no. A month later, an apartment owner returned his call to say that an apartment had become available. Ralph's wife answered the phone. She told the apartment owner that Ralph was no longer interested in finding an apartment, and at that point she agreed to go for marriage counseling.

When I asked Ralph what he had learned, he said he had discovered that for the past four years his wife had not taken his unhappiness with their marriage seriously. The reason was because Ralph was operating at too low a muscle level. As soon as he increased the muscle level by actually looking for an apartment, she took him seriously. They found a good marriage counselor who helped them develop better ways to deal with their differing interests and to negotiate more creative solutions that enhanced rather than damaged their relationship.

I asked Ralph what he would have done differently, knowing what he now knows. He said that he would have increased the muscle level three years earlier. He believes they could have repaired their communication and negotiation problems without having to live through three years of fighting and wear and tear on their relationship.[1]

■　■　■　■

## EXERCISE 4.8
### Using the Appropriate Muscle Level

1. Note a recent situation in which you did not escalate your use of power quickly enough.

2. What were the negative consequences of not using enough power soon enough?

3. What would you do differently next time?


■ ■ ■ ■


## 6. The Power of Taking a Break From the Table

There will be times, in the middle of a negotiation, when you forget to assess how well you are creating and claiming value. Maybe there is a lot of forward momentum, or friendly positive feelings, or you just want to reach a resolution to a long, drawn-out negotiation. You say "yes" to the negotiation and feel good for a short time, and then you notice that you have an uneasy feeling at the bottom of your stomach, and you begin to think, "Maybe I didn't do as well as I should have," or worse, "I think I've been had."

Let me share with you an example of a situation in which I did not negotiate as well as I could have or should have.

My wife, who is a physician, and I had been considering buying a cellular phone to take the place of the beeper that notifies her, when she is "on call," that patients would like to see her or talk with her. It seemed that the cellular phone would be more convenient, but we had been hesitating due to the extra expense. It occurred to us that if the cellular phone also worked at our cottage in the country, it would bring a greater sense of security there.

The salesperson from "Cansell" told us that their phone would work in that area, so I used it to call a neighbor who lives near our cottage. The phone worked perfectly, and I signed the contract.

Later on, I learned that the regional transmitter was powerful enough for the cellular phone to receive calls at our cottage; however, the phone was not powerful enough to send outgoing calls. The salesperson told us that it really wasn't a problem; it had happened before. They would simply install an antenna on our cottage and the phone would work perfectly. After patiently waiting for two months, we were told that it wouldn't work after all. What were our options? If we installed a land phone at the cottage, could they add value in some other way? Could we have a car phone that was light enough for Lynn to use on call? No problem. We tried another phone. It worked perfectly in our car but was too heavy to be of any use when Lynn was on call.

What were my interests? I wanted a working phone at our cottage. If the "Cansell" phone would not work there, I wanted a refund, or I wanted "Cansell" to add value in some other way. I wanted the situation resolved quickly, and I wanted to be treated courteously. It was now three months after our purchase of the phone, and none of my interests were being met. What was my BATNA?

- I could continue to negotiate with "Cansell," even though I had written them several times and had sent them copies of past correspondence but had not received a reply.
- I could take "Cansell" to small claims court.
- I could stop my monthly payments and see if that would bring "Cansell" back to the table.

I received no word from "Cansell," so I stopped making my monthly payments. Finally, I received a letter from a collection agency asking us to pay the back payments or the phone would be repossessed and I would be responsible for paying out the lease minus the amount that "Cansell" could receive for selling the used phone.

Next, I received a telephone call from the collection agency. I had never been in that position before, and I expected that the agency representative would be aggressive and argumentative. Instead, I found myself talking to a very sympathetic woman with a gentle, empathic, kind voice. She told me that "Cansell" was very anxious to settle this matter. (By this time, so was I.) She said that $500 was the lowest amount for which she was authorized to sell me the phone and void the contract. Could she have the courier pick up the check from me today? I said yes, feeling relieved to have the situation settled.

The feeling of relief was short-lived, and then I realized that I had been had. I had spent hours trying to resolve this situation. I mostly likely could have claimed more value. I could have offered her $400 for the phone. After all, I had already paid $198 in monthly installments.

I had said "yes" at the table. I quickly realized that if I had taken a break from the table and said that I would call her back in five minutes I could have negotiated more effectively. After all, I had a strong BATNA. I could have taken "Cansell" to small claims court.

However, I did learn an important lesson, which was not to say "yes" at the negotiating table without taking a break. During this break, assess yourself for creating and claiming value. I didn't fully realize it at the time, but I also had another option. I could have claimed more value before the courier came to pick up the check. I could have reopened the negotiation.

If you find that you have made a mistake in your negotiations, either reopen the negotiation or note in writing what you learned from it and what you will do differently next time. The other option is to beat yourself up and berate yourself for not doing as good as job as you could have, but the only result of this option is a lower sense of self-esteem.

▧ ▧ ▧ ▧

**EXERCISE 4.9**
**Taking Appropriate Breaks From the Table**

1. In the space below, outline a negotiation in which you did not do as well as you could have.

2. Next, describe how a break from the table and/or reopening the negotiation could have helped you to negotiate more effectively.

▧ ▧ ▧ ▧

## 7. The Power of Balance

In negotiating, as in sports and in the justice system, we need to pay close attention to the power of balance. In sporting events, we get a better tennis match between two opponents who are equally skilled or a better hockey game between two teams who are equal matched. A better debate will occur if the two debaters are equally articulate and equally well-informed. Likewise, justice seems more fair when the punishment suits the crime; the outcome is then seen as fair and legitimate. Maintaining balance is a tool that skillful negotiators use effectively, as the following two examples illustrate.

I felt that it was time to buy a new car. The first negotiation involved convincing my wife that we needed it. Our first step was to decide on a make and model. I wanted the top-of-the-line model, partly for the sun roof, partly for the increased horsepower, and—to be honest—partly for the status. My wife wanted something much less extravagant. To help us figure out our options objectively, we used a weighted averaging system.

Based on this analysis, we decided that the best solution was to buy the model I wanted or one model down, only one or two years old, in very good condition and with low mileage. Our present car was good enough for at least one more year, although it needed a fair amount of work. Keeping our present car for the coming year became our BATNA—we could wait. Time was on our side, and we could use it to study the market and even make a few mistakes (e.g., underbid) while we were getting to know the bargaining range for the makes and models we were interested in. We looked at several cars that fit our criteria. We bid on a low-mileage demo with a high price tag, but our bid was too low and the asking price too high to continue that particular negotiation.

We knew and liked the people at the local "ABC" car dealership—in fact, we had bought our last four cars there. We told the sales manager what we were looking for in a relatively new car, in good condition, and with low mileage. One day, a salesperson from the "ABC" dealership called. They had found a car that met most of our criteria. It had been reserved for the owner of the dealership, who was semiretired. Since he spent the winters in Florida, the car had never been exposed to road salt, which causes such damage to cars during the Canadian winters. All of the necessary accessories were already installed (e.g., mud flaps and carpet mats). The car also had a CD player, which made driving it very much like driving a symphony orchestra. There were several drawbacks for me, however. It was not a top-of-the-line car, so there was no sun roof, no extra horsepower, and there was also less status.

I found a brand-new car just like it, only it was the top-of-the-line model. The difference in price was $4,000. That car was clearly not worth the higher price to us. Besides, a one-year-old car with highway mileage would be a better car in the long run than a new one that had been used mostly for stop-and-start city driving.

We called *Consumer Reports,* which gave us a reasonable price range for the car we were now interested in buying and a reasonable selling price for our old car. This use of objective criteria could help correct any misassumptions we had about the worth of the new car and the worth of our old one. With this knowledge in hand, we made an offer on the new car.

I didn't want to play their offer high; I offer low game. I came in with what I thought was a reasonable offer based on our conversation with *Consumer Reports.* The salesperson said it sounded too low but that he would have to talk it over with his sales manager. He came back saying that my offer was too low and that I would have to give him something more to take to his sales manager. I said that I had to stay at that price; my wife would not agree to spending any more money on the car. (The principle of balance came into effect here. The car salesman had to get the approval of his sales manager, and I had to get the approval of my wife.) I reiterated that my research indicated $16,000 to be a fair price for the new car, along with the trade-in of my old car.

Through active listening, I heard him say that he would need to take something to his sales manager. I gave the salesman my credit card number and said that I would be pleased to place a $2,500 deposit on the new car. The salesman came back and said that the sales manager could not accept my offer himself but would be glad to take my offer to the general manager. I reiterated that I had been a loyal customer for the past six years and wanted to be able to continue to have my new car serviced at their dealership.

The salesman came back and accepted my offer, although he didn't like it. It is interesting to note, however, that the salesman said they all had agreed that they had wives to deal with, and on that basis they had accepted my offer (the need to save face).

We got the car we wanted at a good price. The dealership got four more years of our car being serviced by them, which ensured that the car would remain under warranty. The power of balance had been a very helpful tool. The used car manager had to consult with the general manager before he could say yes. I had to consult with my wife before I could say yes.

■ ■ ■ ■

### EXERCISE 4.10
### Using the Power of Balance

Give an example of a negotiation in which you used the power of balance to equalize the power of the parties.

■ ■ ■ ■

Some of my clients have asked to meet the person in the back room either during the negotiation or afterward. The consensus is that sometimes there really is someone in the back room, and sometimes there isn't. An interesting strategy is to state that you want to talk with the person with the actual power to make the decision. Sometimes it works, and you will be able to meet the person in the back room; sometimes it doesn't. In a sense, it doesn't matter, for even if you don't meet the person in the back room, you can even up the decision-making power on your side. You can say you have to confer with someone else, even if that person is yourself. By doing this, you have given yourself an opportunity to take a break from the table, and you have balanced the power in the decision-making process.

The second example illustrates the principle of balance in an assault case involving a 14-year-old boy named Neil. Neil was a member of a local swim team. One day after practice, Neil was in the shower room. When he started to wash his hair, he realized that he had left his shampoo at home. He borrowed what he thought was one of the other team member's shampoo and proceeded to wash his hair. Unfortunately, the shampoo belonged to Fred, a 53-year-old man who also swam at the sports center. Upon seeing

Neil using his shampoo, Fred flew into a rage and slapped Neil across the face hard enough to result in a welt and contusion to his lip.

The coach and the other swimmers were in the locker room by this time. They heard the slap and ran into the shower room just as Fred was making a hasty exit. The manager of the sports center was alerted, and he notified Neil's mother. The manager and the coach also notified the police.

The assault could have resulted in charges being pressed. The manager of the center hoped that this would not happen, as the resulting publicity could damage the excellent reputation that the sports center had in the community. (This was one of the center's primary interests.) At the time, Neil's mother did not want to press charges because she felt that prolonging the incident was not in her son's best interests.

The police tracked down Fred and told him that they viewed the incident and his behavior seriously. He apologized to the police and was told that charges would not be pressed.

Upon hearing that Fred apologized to the police and not to her son, Neil's mother felt a sense of injustice. She said that her son no longer felt completely safe at the sports center and that other team members felt the same way. Neil's mother is a personal friend of mine, knows of my interest in negotiation, and asked for my advice.

I applied the principle of balance. The assault had occurred in a public place, and the sound of the slap and Neil's bleeding lip were witnessed publicly by the coach and team members. As well, Neil and his teammates felt somewhat traumatized by this incident. The principle of balance would indicate that a public apology to Neil in front of his coach and team members was warranted. In this case, Neil's mother also has excellent leverage. Her BATNA was to press charges, which helped bring about the settlement she wanted. She also realized, rightly, that this was a teachable moment for her son and his teammates. She wanted them to see that the system works and that it is legitimate and fair. If a team member assaulted another team member, there would be a legitimate, fair, and equitable consequence for engaging in violent behavior. She rightly thought that the same standard should apply to adults who use the sports center. She also asked that the center revoke Fred's membership if he were to engage in additional acts of physical abuse.

In both of the above stories, the power of balance was used as a tool to even up the process as well as to help insure a fair, equitable, and legitimate outcome.

■  ■  ■  ■

## EXERCISE 4.11
### Using the Power of Balance

1. Describe a negotiation in which you should have used the power of balance but did not.

2. What would you do differently if you had the chance to renegotiate the above situation?

■  ■  ■  ■

### 8. The Power of an Apology

All negotiators lose it at one time or another. Therefore, you have to expect that negotiations get off track and break down. Sometimes, it is your fault, sometimes, the other party's fault, and often, both parties contribute. One of the fundamental differences between professional negotiators and their amateur counterparts is that good negotiators have better skills at getting the negotiation back on track so they can determine if the conflict could and should be resolved or if they are better off going with their BATNA.

One of the most powerful tools a negotiator can use is the power of an apology. Consider the following story, which appears in the *Negotiation Journal* (Goldberg, Green, & Snider, 1987).

> In my first-year Contracts class, I wished to review various doctrines we had recently studied. I put forth the following:
>
> > In a long-term installment contract, seller promises buyer to deliver widgets at the rate of 1,000 a month. The first two deliveries are perfect. However, in the third month seller delivers only 990 widgets. Buyer becomes so incensed that he rejects deliveries and refuses to pay for the widgets already delivered.

After stating the problem, I asked, "If you were Seller, what would you say?" What I was looking for was a discussion of the various common law theories which would force the buyer to pay for the widgets delivered and those which would throw buyer into breach for canceling the remaining deliveries. In short, I wanted the class to come up with the legal doctrines which would allow Seller to crush Buyer.

After asking the question, I looked around the room for a volunteer. As is so often the case with first year students, I found that they were all either writing in their notebooks or inspecting their shoes. There was, however, one eager face, that of an eight-year-old son of one of my students. It seems that he was suffering through Contracts due to his mother's sin of failing to find a sitter. Suddenly he raised his hand. Such behavior, even from an eight-year-old, must be rewarded.

"OK," I said. "What would you say if you were the seller?"

"I'd say, 'I'm sorry.' " (p. 221)

This story illustrates the power of an apology. All of us learned how to apologize as children, but many of us as adults have lost sight of the power of an apology. The following example demonstrates the power of an apology to help change a long-term negative working relationship into a positive one.

Ed is a very successful benefits consultant. Benefits is a complicated field and when an organization is trying to decide on a package of benefits (e.g., health, drug, dental, short-term disability, and long-term disability), it often hires a benefits consultant to select the vendor or vendors who offer the best overall package. In his job as benefits consultant, Ed must negotiate with his clients to determine their interests and priorities and then must negotiate with the various vendors to determine how they can best meet those interests and priorities. Based on this research, he makes recommendations to his clients.

To do his job effectively, Ed must get a great deal of timely information from the vendors. Ed was having difficulty with Joan, from "Health Benefits Inc." Ed and Joan had never had a particularly good working relationship. Recently, that relationship had deteriorated further, thereby marginalizing both Ed and Joan's overall effectiveness in their jobs.

The situation came to a head when Ed and Joan had a quarrel over the phone, which left Ed feeling upset, unsettled, and frustrated. Ed had recently taken a course on the "Getting to Yes" method. He decided to use the method and the "power of the apology" to see if he could develop a more effective working relationship with Joan.

Ed called Joan the next day. He opened the conversation by saying, "If I had yesterday to live over again I would not have come on as strongly as I did." He also stated that he felt he was at least half responsible for their problem in communicating. Ed took a deep breath and waited for Joan's reaction, which turned out to be very positive. Joan stated that she also would be willing to accept half of the responsibility for their problems in communication and that she also was feeling uptight about their working relationship (note that by each of them accepting responsibility for their problems in communicating they had reached their first agreement early in the negotiation).

Ed then told Joan that she was a very important person to him in the running of his consulting practice and that her organization was important to Ed's firm in being able to provide services to his clients. Ed then suggested that the next time he was in Joan's city that they take some time to discuss their relationship over the past few years and how to improve it. Joan readily agreed.

The outcome of this meeting was a vastly improved working relationship. In the past, both had felt pressured by the other. They both agreed that they wanted to replace being pressured with being respectfully persuaded. Joan told Ed that simply because he had opened up the conversation during the previous telephone call she had started to feel more comfortable with him. One year later, Ed told me that he now has an excellent working relationship with Joan.

### The Apology as a Break From the Table

There are times when we all lose it. The discussion becomes heated, and we say things we didn't intend to say. The negotiation, if not the relationship, is unraveling fast. An apology, teamed up with a break from the table, can do wonders to get the negotiation moving again. Consider saying something like the following:

> Things have gotten out of hand here. I'm sure that at least half of the problem is my mistake. Let's take a 15-minute break from the table (the negotiation/the discussion) and start again after the break.

This strategy often works because it is disarming: "I'm sure at least half of the problem was my mistake." How can anyone disagree with this? It also changes the tone and tenor of the discussion from adversarial to cooperative. You have also constructed two agreements. You have invited both parties to take responsibility for the present difficulties in the negotiation, and you have agreed to take a break. Both parties can then begin the negotiations fresh and refreshed.

▓ ▓ ▓ ▓

**EXERCISE 4.12**
**Using the Power of the Apology to**
**Get the Negotiation Back on Track**

1. Think of three times when you apologized during the course of a negotiation with the end result being that you furthered the negotiation process.

    a.

    b.

    c.

2. List specific characteristics of situations where apologizing works for you.

3. How could you use an apology more often to resolve problems and build relationships in your future negotiations?

4. Think of three times when you apologized during the course of a negotiation and it worked against you.

    a.

    b.

    c.

5. List specific characteristics of situations where apologizing worked against you.

6. Based on the above, when should you apologize less often in your future negotiations?

■ ■ ■ ■

Sometimes, the situation is so unclear that you don't know if the other person was being difficult or if you were. As an example, here is a situation in which I, by apologizing, was able to gain enough information to make a correct diagnosis as to where the difficulty lay.

The incident occurred while I was the regional manager of a national firm. One of my colleagues at the head office had a friend I will call Stella. Stella and her husband were planning to move to our area because he had accepted a promotion and transfer.

Stella called me to inquire if there were any job openings with our company. I told her that at present there were none but that I would be happy to meet with her when she visited our area. She suggested a time, but I was unavailable to meet then. The next time she would be coming down was Easter weekend. Easter Monday was a holiday. However, my office assistant and I had agreed to do paperwork Easter Monday, so I agreed to meet Stella at 4 pm that day.

Stella and I met as scheduled. I told her that our area was a small, conservative city and that people had to live here several years before they became accepted. In fact, people who came from outside the Maritime provinces were referred to as CFA's (Come From Away's). I suggested that the best way to become known in the city was to work for an agency for several years and build up contacts. I gave her the names of several agencies and the names of the directors of those agencies and their telephone numbers. I also said that if she were to develop a private practice we had extra office space in our centrally located building and would be able to rent it to her part-time at a reasonable price. In short, I thought that I had been the perfect host.

The next thing I heard was that Stella had reported to her friend that I had been "incredibly rude." I was dumbfounded. I decided to call her and apologize—for two reasons: First, I wanted to tell her that my intent was to be helpful, and second, I wanted further data. People in our head office said that Stella was wonderful and had an excellent reputation. I felt that our second interview on the phone would give me more information to help me decide if she was being difficult, or if I was.

When I called her, I apologized for her feeling that I had been rude and told her that my intent had been to be helpful. She was surprised that word of her remarks had reached me. I told her that I too was surprised to hear that she felt that I had been rude. (The fact that both of us were surprised could have created some common ground.) When she recovered from her surprise, she said— and I quote—"You were somewhat helpful."

I now had all the information I needed. I had approached her open-handed and she still had a need to "put me down." She said that she was in the process of leaving her office and would like to call me back, but she never did.

I don't know what was going on with Stella. I suspect that she loved her job and did not want to move. My apology gave me enough data to determine for myself that she was the one who had been "rude" in this situation. Without the apology, I would never have known if it was she or if it was I. In other words, the apology and her reaction to it gave me a sense of closure.

### 9. The Power of Acknowledging Progress

Good negotiators are twice as likely to verbally acknowledge progress during the negotiation. For example, a good negotiator might say "So far, we have worked very hard and have been able to agree on items A, B, and C. Everyone seems very tired now, so why don't we come back tomorrow and tackle items D, E, and F?" Another example is "We did a great job in resolving situations X, Y, and Z. Let's see if we can approach problems R, S, and T with the same amount of creativity and cooperative spirit." Please note that the praise must be genuine and sincere, for if it is at all phony, it will do more harm than good.

## 10. The Power of Debriefing the Negotiation

Effective negotiators are twice as likely to debrief after a negotiation. To do so effectively, the debriefing must be systematic. The following techniques and debriefing forms will help you get salient, focused, in-depth feedback on your negotiation skills and style. These techniques and forms will help you analyze patterns in your negotiation style that work for you as well as those that work against you.

### Before the Negotiation, Estimate Your Chances for Success

There is great value in estimating your probability of success before the negotiation begins and then comparing that estimate with your actual success after the negotiation has concluded. Most of the time there is a discrepancy between these two figures. Your preliminary estimate of "success"—that is, getting what you want from the negotiation—is usually too high. The reason for this is that most people go into negotiations overconfident and underprepared. The following story from Russo and Schoemaker's (1989) book *Decision Traps* illustrates this point:

> It has been reported that an ex-CEO of City Bank in the United States kept a list of the 100 worst loans made by his loan officers. If you were a loan officer at City Bank, the last place you would want your name to appear would be on that list. The list was kept not so much for punitive purposes as for educational ones. The list reminded the bank's loan officers that there were consequences to their actions; therefore, before making a loan, be prudent and estimate carefully the likelihood of that loan being repaid.
>
> When that CEO retired, the practice of keeping a list of the 100 worst loans retired with him. After that, the performance of City Bank's loan officers deteriorated. (p. 100)

The point here is that if you estimate at 90% your chances of getting what you want from a negotiation and your success rate is only 40%, this is salient feedback. It helps you focus on what went wrong. Was your estimate of success too high? Were you not well enough prepared? Were you deceived in the negotiation? Keep the answers to these questions in a log book and look for patterns. If there is a pattern—and there usually is—you can learn from it.

Most people complain that they don't get enough feedback on the job. In truth, the world is a very rich place in terms of feedback. As I have stated, you do have to be more assertive in asking for feedback regarding your negotiation skills and style. You also have to do a better of job of using the feedback that already exists. Estimating your chances of success before a negotiation and seeing how close you come to that estimate is an excellent tool for helping obtain essential feedback to improve your negotiating skills and style.

## The Value of a Negotiation Log

The negotiation log is one of the most useful ways of improving your negotiating skills and style. There are many types of negotiation logs, from very structured to free-form. Rather than argue which is best, my recommendation is to vary the feedback device from time to time. Each of these forms focuses in on different aspects of your style and skills.

In the free-form type of negotiation log, you record any impressions that you have about your negotiations. The advantage of this type of log is that you are not restricted by any particular structure. Looking back after several months of this type of journaling often rewards you with insights and patterns that can be used to negotiate more effectively in the future.

A take-off on this method, if you are comfortable doing it, is to share your journal with a trusted friend. The discussions between you and your friend can often produce additional insights. For example, Michelle found that when the other party tended to withhold information, she did not negotiate as well as she should have. Michelle described herself as going "ballistic" in situations where she had to negotiate with people who withheld information, but she never saw how this negatively affected her ability to negotiate until she debriefed three similar situations with her friend Carol. Michelle then went on to figure out how to negotiate more effectively with people who withheld information. Because people who withhold information are often critical, Michelle, with the help of her log and coaching from her friend Carol, learned to ask her withholding partners in the negotiation to criticize her proposals. In doing so, they were telling her about their interests and priorities. Michelle said that she also learned to be more patient, and although she may not get all the information she needs all at once, by asking high-yield questions and by researching other sources Michelle has learned that she will eventually get most, if not all, of the information she needs to negotiate successfully.

More structured ways to keep a negotiation log involve the use of negotiation feedback forms.

### The Value of Negotiation Feedback Forms

The three forms described here are designed to help you realize the power of pattern analysis and focused feedback. The first one, the *Three-By-Three Feedback Form,* asks you to list three things you did well in the negotiation and three targets for improvement (three things you would do better if you were to redo that particular negotiation).

The reasoning behind asking you to list what you did well is that if you are more conscious of what you are doing well you will tend to do it more often. The focused feedback on what you do well can also give you insight into the most appropriate time to use a particular skill.

By the time you have done this exercise three or four times, clear patterns tend to emerge—patterns of what you are doing well and patterns showing areas where improvement is required.

For example, Lois discovered that by using her excellent listening skills she was doing a very good job of learning about the other party's interests. She also found that she was not doing a good enough job of articulating her interests in the negotiation.

## THREE-BY-THREE FEEDBACK FORM

Name _____

List three things that were done well.

1.


2.


3.

List three targets for improvement.

1.

2.

3.

The second form, the *Two-Party Debriefing Form,* asks you to debrief the negotiating skills of not only the other party but also your own. This form is purposely structured so that you rate the positive and negative aspects of the other party's negotiating style first. The reason for this is that left to our own devices we often talk about what we did not like about the other party and/or their negotiating style. Looking at what the other party did well and areas where you think they could improve gives a more balanced picture.

If it is difficult to be objective about others, it is doubly difficult to be objective about ourselves. By using this form to first be more objective about the other party you are negotiating with makes it more likely that you will be objective about your own negotiating strengths and able to identify areas where improvement is required. Here again, looking at patterns after several months of collecting data provides you with the clearest patterns of your strengths and your targets for improvement. For example, Jim noticed that by analyzing the other party's negotiating skills first, he found that he could be more "objective" in analyzing his own skills. Since the focus of this form is different from the first one, you will tend to learn different things about your negotiating style. It is a good idea to use one form for a while and then switch to another, as each form provides a different type of feedback.

## TWO-PARTY DEBRIEFING FORM

Name _____

1. What did they do right?


2. What should they do differently next time?


3. What did I do right?


4. What would I do differently next time?


The third is the *Hard–Soft–Principled Style Form* from Fisher and Ury's (1981) book *Getting to Yes.* On this form, you are asked to mark the appropriate style (hard/soft/principled) in response to each of 13 statements. For example, George's response was "principled" to all the questions except 5 and 7. By filling out the form after each of his negotiations, he found that he often rated Questions 5 and 7 in the "soft" column. This focused feedback helped George formulate objectives for improving his negotiations in the future.

Warning!! Real change, like aging, takes place slowly. Try one method and stick by it for at least a month. One of the most frequent mistakes some of my students have made was to get very enthusiastic and start tracking their negotiation skills with three separate feedback forms. After two weeks, the task was too demanding—and they stopped collecting feedback. The best advice here is to keep it short and simple.

### Note

1. More and more marriage and family counselors are using the books *Getting to yes* and *Getting past no* as a way to help their clients have a more satisfying domestic life. Both books are listed in the bibliography at the end of this book.

# 5

## Dealing With Difficult People
## and Difficult Situations

■ ■ ■ ■

It has been said that 90% of our stress is a result of dealing with the 4% of the population that we find to be difficult. These are the people whom we can get emotionally hooked. Often, it seems that the harder we try to extricate ourselves from these situations, the more enmeshed we become. The old tale of Brer Rabbit and the tar baby is illustrative of what can happen when you get enmeshed in a difficult situation.

### The "Tar Baby" Effect

One day Brer Fox decided to trap his perennial adversary, Brer Rabbit, by fashioning a likeness of a baby out of tar. Brer Rabbit spotted this "tar baby" by the side of the road and tried to engage it in a bit of friendly conversation. The more Brer Rabbit talked to the tar baby, who of course had nothing to say in return, the angrier he got. "Mawnin'! Nice wedder dis mawnin'," said old Brer Rabbit. No response. "Is you deaf? Kaze ef you is, I kin holler louder." No response. "Ef you don't take off dat hat and tell me howdy, I'm gwine ter bus' you wide open." No response. At last Brer Rabbit could stand it no longer. He punched the tar baby in the nose, only to get his fist stuck and find himself increasingly irate. So he hauled off and hit the tar baby with the other fist, and it too got stuck in the tar. Punch led to kick, and before long Brer Rabbit was completely entangled. Indeed, the harder he tried to extricate himself, the more enmeshed he became. (Pruitt & Rubin, 1986, p. 118)

Negotiating effectively requires that you do not get enmeshed, or if you do, that you quickly extricate yourself—all of which requires a great deal of self-control.

## ■ Developing Self-Control

The first thing you need to do in dealing with a difficult person is not to control that person's behavior but to control your own. To develop better self-control, you first need to define the term. Several expert negotiators have defined self-control as the ability to do the following:

- ■ Keep your emotions in check and not let them override or interfere with your judgment
- ■ Not personalize the situation or the behavior of the other party, which includes realizing that their behavior is not an attack on you personally
- ■ Make rational decisions to behave in a particular way in spite of strong emotional feeling to behave the opposite way

Difficult people and difficult situations are a true test of your negotiating and influencing skills. They also provide one of the best sources of information of what you need to change in order to negotiate more effectively.

## ■ Eight Essential Negotiating Skills

To bring about systematic improvement in your negotiating skills and in your self-control, you need to master the following eight essential skills or powers:

1. Accurate diagnosis
2. Perspective management
3. Knowing core values and core beliefs
4. Effective anger management
5. Doing the unexpected
6. Role selection
7. Looking for reasonable people in unreasonable situations
8. Resiliency

## The Power of an Accurate Diagnosis

When I teach my course "Dealing with Difficult People," I am often asked what I think about the books, workshops, and video presentations that teach us to diagnose the difficult person as to type, for example: the "Sherman tank" (for aggressives), the "grenade thrower" (for passive-aggressives), the chronic complainer, wet blanket, know-it-all, and the superagreeable. Some of the prescribed strategies work some of the time; however, there are several fundamental flaws in this approach. First, once we have labeled someone, we tend to believe in the truth of the label itself. For example, if we label someone a "Sherman tank," and then they do something "un-Sherman-tank-like," we are less likely to see it and therefore less likely to use it to effectively change the negotiation for the better. Even if we use the more neutral label of "opponent," we are less likely to observe any "un-opponent-like" behavior. Second, we may prematurely label a person because we lack critical information. At one time or another, all of us have been labeled negatively and unfairly by someone who did not fully understand the situation.

I call this phenomenon "premature labeling." We dislike it when it happens to us, and we should be careful not to do it to others. Not only is it unfair, it also makes us less effective as negotiators. There are four rules of thumb for avoiding premature labeling:

- *Rule #1.* Have I observed the same behavior in three similar situations? One time, and it may have been an accident; two times, and it starts to look like a pattern; three times—that is, three instances of the negative behavior in three similar situations—and it probably is a pattern.
- *Rule #2.* Is the other party experiencing exceptional stress? Say, for example, that you have observed Frank behaving in a difficult manner recently in three

similar situations. However, you have also heard that Frank and his wife have recently separated. Frank may very well be suffering from exceptional stress, and that stress may be at the root of his behavior.

- *Rule #3.* Am I experiencing exceptional stress? There have been times when each of us has been under enough stress that it has influenced us to see other people's behavior more negatively than is appropriate.

- *Rule #4.* If you have observed the same "negative" behavior on three separate occasions, and if the other party is not suffering from too much stress, and you are not suffering from too much stress, there is still one more question you have to answer before labeling the other person's behavior as difficult: "Have I had an adult-to-adult conversation with the other party in an effort to resolve the problem and improve the situation?" There are times when the other party may not realize that their behavior is causing a problem for you, and you may be able to negotiate a good solution to the problem during this adult-to-adult conversation.

To summarize, none of us likes to be labeled. All of us have been labeled unfairly by someone else at some point during our lives. One of the best ways to avoid labeling others prematurely is to ask yourself the following four questions:

- Have I seen the same behavior in three similar situations?
- Is the other party experiencing stress that may be influencing his or her behavior?
- Am I suffering any exceptional stress that may be affecting the way I see the world, and more specifically, the way I see the other party's behavior?
- Have I had an adult-to-adult conversation with the other party to see if we can negotiate an effective resolution to the problem?

There is no doubt in my mind that some people are difficult in general. It has been estimated that 4% of the population are generally difficult across a large number of situations.

DIFFICULT PEOPLE BEHAVE IN A DIFFICULT MANNER BECAUSE THEY HAVE LEARNED THAT DOING SO KEEPS YOU OFF BAL-ANCE AND INCAPABLE OF EFFECTIVE ACTION.

It is imperative that you accurately diagnose a situation before you try to treat it. As is said in medicine, "a correct diagnosis is half the cure."

There are basically two types of difficult people. The majority of difficult people are "situationally difficult." They are suffering from exceptional stress, are in a difficult situation, do not have the skills to negotiate more effectively, and/or do not perceive that they have any viable options. Once viable options are "put on the table," their behavior ceases to be difficult.

The other type is the 4% of the population that are difficult across almost all situations. These people behave as they do because it works for them—they get what they want frequently enough to reinforce their negative behavior. They have had years of practice in their families of origin and subsequent practice on countless unsuspecting strangers. If there were an Olympics for difficult behavior, these people would be in contention for the gold, silver, and bronze medals every time.

As expert negotiators, we have to make an accurate diagnosis. There are, however, two types of errors that we can make. First, if we diagnose a situationally difficult person as a perennially difficult person, we risk giving up prematurely, behaving in a difficult manner ourselves, and ending up with a self-fulfilling prophecy: "I thought she was difficult. I overreacted and behaved in a difficult manner myself. She reacted to my being difficult and became more difficult. I reacted to her becoming more difficult by becoming more adversarial." If only we had asked the right question at the right time or shared a piece of information that we chose to withhold, the outcome of the negotiation would have been entirely different—maybe even entirely satisfactory.

The other type of error we can make is continually trying to negotiate with people who will not or cannot change. We fall into the trap of blaming ourselves and thinking that if only we were more skillful, things would have been different; and we continually ask advice from others (until they start to label us as difficult).

Sometimes, we hang in there for years after we should have quit. Finally, we realize that we have used up two years of emotional energy and have received "nothing" in return. In cases like this, learning when not to negotiate and to go with our BATNA instead can be the most important lesson that we need to learn.

To help determine which type of negotiation you are in, describe as specifically as possible what the other party does that makes it difficult for you to negotiate effectively. What does the "difficult person" do to keep you off balance? Some of the behaviors of "difficult people" are the following: aggressive, passive, passive-aggressive, loud, swearing, shouting, lying, not listening, name calling, threatening to go to one's supervisor, belittling, withholding relevant information, being abusive in public, being persistent, and/or not letting you speak.

Beside carefully observing how the other party behaves, you need to figure out what they need or want. Some of the things that difficult people want are control, power, attention, to "be right," and ego status. By carefully figuring out what the other party wants, you are in a better position to negotiate effectively with them because it may be very easy for you to give them some of what they want and much less likely that you will get "emotionally hooked." The topic of protecting yourself from getting emotionally hooked and getting yourself unhooked once you are is covered more fully later in this chapter in the sections "The Power of Knowing Your Core Beliefs" and "The Power of Knowing Your Core Values."

You also are in a much better position to negotiate with the other person when you can see clearly both your behavior and theirs. An excellent way to do this is to clearly describe in writing how you perceive the problem. For example, Joan describes the problems she is having with her supervisor Rosemary as follows:

> I am usually a very highly motivated worker. The quality of my work has always been appreciated by my supervisors and my peers, until Rosemary became my supervisor. When she assigns tasks and projects to me, I try to ask her how the project fits into the larger scheme of the work and how the project relates to our departmental objectives. I can work harder and do a better job if I have a better sense of the underlying purpose of the projects I work on. When I ask Rosemary for a more detailed explanation of the purpose of a project, she becomes quite curt, revealing very little information. After eight months of this type of treatment, I am worried that I am not as motivated as I once was or would like to be.

Next, write down as clearly as possible how you perceive that the other person sees the problem. This is critically important. As Roger Fisher states, "You are not in a position to change someone's mind [their perception of the situation] unless you first know what their perception of the problem is." For example, when I interviewed Rosemary concerning the problems she and Joan were having, Rosemary stated,

> Joan is a very good worker, but I find her too aggressive. She keeps asking about things that are not part of her job. I shared some of this information with her at first but recently have been reluctant to say more. I really think

she views herself as more competent than I am. In my heart of hearts, I think she wants my job.

Given that Joan and Rosemary have made the above assumptions, it is no wonder they have trouble understanding and communicating with each other.

An excellent way to do this is to actually write out a piece of the dialogue you had with the "difficult" person. One approach to this is to divide a page in half by drawing a vertical line down one side. In the right-hand column, write down the initials of the parties and the corresponding dialogue. Then go back and write down in the left-hand column what you thought and/or felt at each part of the dialogue. This exercise is guaranteed to help you gain insight into the behavior of both participants—you and your "difficult" party. Armed with this insight, you are in a position to negotiate more effectively.

### The Power of Perspective Management

Perspective management is your first line of defense against losing your self-control in dealing with difficult people. Perspective management protects you from becoming emotionally hooked, or if you get hooked, it helps you keep your psychological distance. The following story illustrates the concept of perspective management.

The story begins on the day Dan Rather was selected to be the new anchorperson on the CBS evening news, replacing Walter Cronkite, who was about to retire. How did Dan feel when he heard that he was the successful candidate? Mixed feelings. Of course, he was happy to be selected, but he also felt his stress level go up. Walter Cronkite was the most popular anchorperson in the history of television broadcasting. Ninety-two percent of the U.S. population would have voted for Cronkite for president. The Nielson ratings (percentage of the viewing public who watch each program) were scheduled for publication at the end of the month. The rating for the CBS evening news would either increase, decrease, or stay the same. The most likely scenario was that the ratings would decrease. For the first time in years, the viewing public, loyal to Walter Cronkite, was expected to change dials to see what the other channels had to offer. NBC and ABC would like to make the most of this unique opportunity. What happened to Dan Rather's stress level? It went up.

On the day that Dan started his job as the news anchor at CBS, he was determined to do the best job possible. He and his team picked the best of the 20,000 stories that come into the newsroom each day, and they edited them to the second. At 5 p.m., Dan went out for some refreshments. Returning to his desk at 5:30, he found the news team in a panic. A news bulletin had just arrived saying that President Reagan had been shot. The whole day's work had to be thrown out. Four new stories had to be ready for the 6:30 pm telecast: How was the president's health? Who shot the president? Who was in charge of the government? What would be the ramifications on gun control from the shooting? There was not enough time to adequately prepare any of these stories, but there was no choice. What happened to Dan Rather's stress level? It went up again.

At 6:30, he began the telecast with "Good evening. This is Dan Rather with the CBS evening news. Our lead story tonight is that President Reagan has been shot." Suddenly, there was a flash of light above the #1 camera. Brownish, blackish, burnt-rubber-smelling smoke slowly wafted up toward the ceiling. The teleprompter—which had worked perfectly for the past five years—was 100% dead. What happened to Dan Rather's stress level? It went up again.

During an interview several years later, in which Dan related this story, he was asked how he dealt with that much stress. His response was that he took a deep breath and said to himself, "There are 800 million adult Chinese who don't give a damn about this broadcast." In spite of the tremendous stress, he used perspective management to keep things in perspective. If you are going to negotiate effectively, you also must keep things in perspective.

A proven method to help you regain your perspective after you have lost it is it to analyze how your core values and core beliefs have been psychologically hooked and to examine where your core values and beliefs work for you and where they work against you.

■ ▓ ▓ ▓

**EXERCISE 5.1**
**The Power of Perspective Management**

In the space below, describe three situations in which you successfully used perspective management and kept your perspective when negotiating with a difficult person or in negotiating a difficult situation:

1.

2.

3.

■ ■ ■ ■

**EXERCISE 5.2**
**The Cost of Not Using Perspective Management**

In the space below, describe three situations in which you were not
successful in using perspective management and you lost your perspective when negotiating with a difficult person or in a difficult situation:

1.

2.

3.

■ ■ ■ ■

**EXERCISE 5.3**
**Using Perspective Management More Effectively**

In reviewing these six situations, what have you learned about perspective management that will help you to keep your perspective and negotiate more effectively in the future?

■ ■ ■ ■

## The Power of Knowing Your Core Values

In negotiating and in dealing with difficult people, I frequently hear phrases like "She presses my hot buttons every time, so I continually lose it with her!" The problem with the phrase "hot buttons" is that rarely does anyone stop to think what this phrase refers to.

The phrase "hot buttons" refers to your core beliefs and core values. Once these beliefs and/or values are hooked, you are likely to react as follows:

* Lose your perspective
* Become angry, hurt, or defensive
* Make nonvigilant decisions (underreact by not saying or doing what needs to be said or done)
* Make hypervigilant decisions (overreact by saying or doing things that should not be said or done)

All of the above will cause you to negotiate less effectively than you would like. In learning to negotiate effectively, there are two basic points to remember: Keep your perspective and keep your self-control. There are also two essential points to remember in order to negotiate a successful outcome: Know what your core values and core beliefs are and know where they work for you and where they work against you.

The first step is to define the term "core values." Core values are deeply held values that govern how you behave across a great many situations. Core values are powerful because they generate feelings, thoughts, and behavior. A negative example of a core value is guilt. Perhaps Erma Bombeck expressed it best when she said that "guilt is a gift that parents can give their children that keeps on giving."

Here is an example. My mother was very frugal. In the home where I grew up, my mother's core value of being frugal expressed itself in her injunction to turn off the lights and to not waste food and in being very reluctant to call long distance on the telephone.

Thirty years later, as a "mature" middle-aged man, I received a message from my answering service concerning an invitation for me to teach a seminar on "Effective Negotiating and Customer Service Skills" for a multinational firm in Toronto. All I must do is call them back (long distance) to say that I will be available on the dates they desire for the course. The firm will pay me more money per day than I have ever earned before. I pick up the phone to return the call. I dial "1" for long distance before the area code "416." This raises an interesting question: How do I feel between the "1" and the "416"? One option is proud, happy, and successful because I am calling to close a deal on a very good contract. The other option is guilty because of an internalized core value that I learned as a child about the use of long-distance telephone calls. In this case, a core value of being frugal, 30 years later, still generates feelings of guilt.

Core values can also be positive, as in the following. There was a story on the evening news about a 16-year-old young man in the Midwest. His father had recently died of ALS (amyotrophic lateral sclerosis, commonly known as Lou Gehrig's disease). His family donated their family van, equipped with a wheelchair lift, to a charitable car auction. The funds raised from the car auction would go to medical research.

The young man had worked all summer long to finance the purchase of his first car, which he had planned to buy at the same auction. The bidding had started on his family's van. A woman who also had ALS bid on the van. Unfortunately, she had to drop out after the bidding reached the limit of her funds. The young man in our story noticed this and continued the bidding, sacrificing the money he had earned for his own car so the woman would be able to have transportation. Obviously, the positive core value in this case was altruism.

I now turn to how core values can affect the negotiating process.

As a negotiator, you need to know what your core values are so that you can develop control over them rather than letting them control you. For example, perhaps one of your core values is being polite, and a salesperson is rude to you. If you automatically become angry and attack the salesperson without first thinking about an appropriate strategy, your core value of politeness has been hooked, and you become a reactive negotiator rather than a proactive one.

### How Do You Discover What Your Core Values Are?

One of the best methods of discovering what your core values are is to keep a log of the "difficult people" you encounter. For each episode you encounter with a "difficult person" and/or a "difficult situation," write a brief description in your log. At the end of your description, identify the core value or values that were hooked for you.

Here is an example. My company won a contract to deliver a high-level training program for Organization "ABC," who turned out to be very demanding. Shortly after we had arrived at a detailed understanding of what they wanted in the workshop, we received a telephone call from them asking us to make major changes. At the time, we felt that this was a very important contract, and we dutifully made every change. However, by the end of the design period, I was feeling very frustrated. What were the core values that were being hooked on my part?

- Desire to do a good job
- A strong desire to please the customer

Once you have analyzed your core values, you are ready to move on to Step 2.

In this step, you carefully examine where your core values work for you and where they work against you. My core values that I described above—to do a good job and to please the customer —have helped me develop a very good reputation. However, in the case cited, I spent so much time trying to please this particular client, for no additional fees, that I did not have time to pursue other work, and in that yearly financial quarter my firm did less well than it otherwise would have.

As core values are an extremely important tool in helping you diagnose your own behavior, and as it can be a difficult concept to grasp, I offer one more example:

Dorothy Smith is a very loyal person. One of her strongest core values is loyalty. Because she is so loyal, she still has very good friends from elementary school. She has friends from work and friends from the neighborhood. Because Dorothy has earned such a large number of loyal friends, she is able to ask their help when she needs it, and this has proved advantageous both personally and professionally. In these cases, the core value of loyalty has worked very well in Dorothy's life.

Dorothy has worked for the same boss for the past 15 years. He is one of the most miserable people to work for in the country—high expectations and little or no acknowledgment, recognition, reward, or opportunity for advancement. In this case Dorothy's core value of loyalty is not only not appreciated, it is misguided. Dorothy should have looked for more suitable and rewarding employment long ago. Therefore, in this situation, Dorothy's core value of loyalty is working against her.

There will be times when you have analyzed a situation and you just can't seem to pinpoint the core value. Often, this happens because you are too close to the situation. Explaining the situation to a trusted and insightful friend can help you "see" the previously hidden core value.

■  ■  ■  ■

**EXERCISE 5.4**
**Identification of Core Values**

1. In the space provided, briefly describe a situation that was difficult for you.

Was there a core value(s) that had me hooked in this particular negotiation? If so, name the core value(s):

_____    _____

_____

If you need help in identifying the core value(s), who would be a good person(s) to contact?

_____    _____

Last, how do you need to modify the way you use this core value to ensure that it continues to work for you in those situations where it should and keep you from using it in situations where it has worked against you?

2. Briefly describe a situation that was difficult for you.

Was there a core value(s) that had you hooked in this particular negotiation? If so, name the core value(s):

_____     _____

_____

If you need help in identifying the core value(s), who would be a good person(s) to contact?

_____     _____

Last, how do you need to modify the way you use this core value to ensure that it will continue to work for you in those situations where it should and keep you from using it in situations where it has worked against you?


3. Briefly describe a situation that was difficult for you.


Was there a core value(s) that had you hooked in this particular negotiation? If so, name the core value(s):

_____     _____

_____

If you need help in identifying the core value(s), who would be a good person(s) to contact?

_____     _____

Last, do you need to modify the way you use one or more of the core value(s) identified in this exercise to ensure that they will work for you in those situations where they should and keep you from using them in situations where they have worked against you?

■ ■ ■ ■

**EXERCISE 5.5**
**Modifying Core Values**

1. List the core values you have identified that need to be modified.

2. How do they need to be modified so you can negotiate more effectively?

■ ■ ■ ■

### The Power of Knowing Your Core Beliefs

Core beliefs are very similar to core values. Core beliefs are deeply held psychological beliefs that govern how you behave across a great many situations. As was stated earlier, it is difficult to gain insight into what your core values and core beliefs are. This section looks at a tool, the Core Beliefs Identification Sheet, that can help you articulate your core beliefs.

When you find yourself ruminating about a situation—that is, going over the situation again and again—it is often an indication that one of your core values or core beliefs is caught. The psychologist Albert Ellis based a great deal of his school of psychotherapy, Rational-Emotive Therapy, on helping people examine their core beliefs and decide more consciously whether or not they apply in specific situations. For example, three of the primary self-defeating beliefs that he (Ellis & Harper, 1975) named are these:

- I must be perfect.
- People should approve of me.
- Life must be fair.

Think about a situation in which you were emotionally hooked. Then complete the Core Beliefs Identification Inventory presented in Exercise 5.6. If you complete this inventory for situations in which you were emotionally hooked in the past and/or for new situations when they arise, the chances are good that you will see that the same core beliefs keep turning up. Awareness is the first step along the road to positive change.

▧ ▧ ▧ ▧

## EXERCISE 5.6
### Identification of Core Beliefs

- I must be loved or accepted by everyone.
- I must be perfect in all I do.
- All the people with whom I work or live must be perfect.
- I can have little control over what happens to me.
- It is easier to avoid facing difficulties and responsibilities than to deal with them.
- Disagreement and conflict should be avoided at all costs.
- People, including me, do not change.
- Some people are always good; others are always bad.
- The world should be perfect, and it is terrible and catastropher when it is not.
- People are fragile and need to be protected from "the Truth."
- Other people exist to make me happy, and cannot be happy unless others make me happy.
- Crises are invariably destructive, and no good can come from them.
- Somewhere there is the perfect job, the perfect "solution," the perfect partner, and so on, and all I need to do is search for them.
- I should not have problems. If I do, it indicates I am incompetent.
- There is one and only one way of seeing any situation—the "true" way.

Remember the last time you felt bad about something? What were you telling yourself? Were any of these 15 beliefs the basis for your self-talk?

Now, you are going to challenge the destructive self-talk that caused you those difficulties. For the event you have just thought about, write down your self-destructive talk in your own words. It may well include self-condemnation and be full of what people should or ought to do. (Appendix B contains an additional copy for future use.)

## MY SELF-DEFEATING BELIEF

The event:

What I felt:

What I was telling myself:

What I did:

What my self-defeating belief(s) was (were):

Now, you are going to challenge your negative self-talk. You can challenge that negative core belief by re-interpreting it and by exchanging the shoulds and oughts for preferences for how you would like things to be. Or you can ask yourself what you can learn from that experience and how you could behave differently next time by filling in the table below.

My constructive self-talk would be:

My feelings would be:

My actions could be:

■  ■  ■  ■

Author's Note: This exercise was adapted from Ellis and Harper (1975).

Here is a situation in which this inventory was used. The case involved an employee, Rob, who thought his new manager, Warren, was less than honest about an important piece of information concerning some changes in the company that would directly affect Rob's position. When Rob confronted his manager with the specifics of the incident, Warren denied having any knowledge of the changes.

Rob was planning to confront his manager a second time because he felt that establishing trust between them early on would help make their working relationship more productive. Before confronting Warren, Rob filled out the Core Beliefs Identification Inventory to help him see if any of his core beliefs were hooked. This exercise helped Rob see that he was indeed emotionally hooked at Core Belief 3: "All the people with whom I work or live must be perfect." Rob told me that he wanted to be sure that he led his core values rather than them controlling him. He then tried a much softer, more controlled confrontation with his new manager. Rob told me that he wanted to be able to see himself, his manager, and the situation as clearly as possible, and the softer, more controlled confrontation would help him do just that.

Before Rob started using this inventory to help unhook himself, he knew that he had difficulty from time to time in trying to be a perfectionist. The inventory helped him see that he was using perfectionistic standards with others, too. Rob's final comment to me was that sometimes the most interesting and difficult negotiations are the ones we have with ourselves.

## The Power of Appropriate Anger Management

"I gave the best speech I regretted when I was angry."

Each of us can cite examples of situations in which we allowed ourselves to become so angry that we damaged the negotiation to the point where "value" was left on the table, and/or we damaged a relationship that was important to us. In cases like this, too much anger and/or too much uncontrolled anger resulted in our making nonvigilant or hypervigilant decisions, which negatively affected both the process of the negotiation and its outcome.

Statistical research indicates that one-third of all automobile accidents occur when the driver is angry. Inappropriate expression of anger contributes not only to car accidents, but also to ruined negotiations. It is imperative, therefore, that good negotiators know how to both manage and express anger appropriately.

This section first looks at techniques for effectively managing anger and then looks at how to use anger appropriately in the negotiating process.

Some of the techniques that aid in effective anger management are perspective management, talking out the problem with someone outside the negotiation, taking a cooling-off break, and writing down actions to be taken at each muscle level so you do not escalate too soon or too quickly. These techniques have been explained earlier in this book.

The Anger Management Form (Exercise 5.7) can also help you process your anger in a way that is more likely to be effective.

**EXERCISE 5.7**
**Anger Management Form**

1. How intense am I going to allow my anger to become?

2. How long am I going to stay angry?

3. How am I going to use my anger constructively?

Here is an example of how this technique was used. Craig has a small computer firm that specializes in selling and servicing computer networks to hospitals. Due to the increased use of technology, his business has done well over the past seven years. One of his first customers was "Main Street General Hospital." At the time this story began, Main Street Hospital was about to integrate all its computers onto a single integrated network. This was a big and important project for the hospital. Craig thought he had the inside lead since he had serviced the hospital for seven years and was well liked and trusted by the hospital staff. Also, the hospital had had several major emergencies with its personal computers during those seven years, and Craig had always been called in when the problems were too difficult for the hospital staff to solve. For example, in several cases, a disk drive had completely stopped working; unfortunately, no backup of essential medical information existed, and Craig had worked for 24 hours straight to successfully retrieve the data.

Craig was invited to bid for the "network" project along with several other vendors. A short list of three vendors, including Craig, was announced. Two weeks later, the winner of the contract was announced. Much to his surprise, it was not Craig. As part of the proposal process, all the vendors had been required to give three references of other network installations their companies had successfully implemented. None of Craig's references had been contacted by the hospital committee responsible for selecting the vendor. There was some speculation that a hospital board member was very supportive of the winning bidder. Craig was livid. Not only did the process seemed flawed and biased, not only were his references not checked, but the "heroic" work that he had put in at the hospital seemed to have been completely ignored.

Craig came to see me because he was in a moral dilemma. On the one hand, he felt unfairly treated. On the other hand, if he complained, it could be perceived as "sour grapes" and could damage his reputation with Main Street Hospital and with other hospitals in the community. Craig said that he thought about the "unfairness" of the situation all the time. It was interfering with his concentration. He had other work to do and other projects to bid on, but he was so angry that he couldn't get back into it. I suggested that, to process this type of anger effectively, he complete the Anger Management Form. Here are Craig's responses to the form's three questions:

1. *How intense are you going to allow your anger to become?*

I asked Craig the "scaling question" from Brief Solution-Focused Therapy. This question asked him to imagine a scale running from 1 to 10. If point 1 on the scale represents absolute calm and point 10 represents absolute rage, at the point he found out that he was not awarded the contract, where was he on the scale? Craig said that he was at a 6 or 7. I asked him where he was on the scale when he found out that his references had not been called. Craig said that he was at an 8 or 9. At the time of our interview, which was a little over a year after not being awarded the contract, I asked Craig where he would be on the scale, and he said 5. The scaling question clearly gives a great deal of information about how angry a person is. It also enables you to rank the degree of anger relative to specific events and to "measure" changes in the degree of anger over time. In other situations, a person's reponse to the question "How intense are you going to allow your anger to become?" provides sufficient information so that the scaling part of the question is not necessary.

2. *How long are you going to stay angry?*

Craig answered, "I have been upset about losing this contract for over a year. I know it is foolish for me to continue to be upset, but I just can't seem to shake it. I feel that I was treated very poorly." I asked Craig how much longer he wanted to stay angry, and he said that he wanted to get over his angry feelings immediately. This told me that the time was right for Craig to let go of these angry feelings; we just needed to find the right mechanism to help him do it. I hoped that the next question would be that mechanism.

3. *How are you going to use your anger constructively?*

Craig decided that he would become much more proactive in the area of marketing. He would develop a company brochure. He would elicit letters of recommendation from previous clients and all current clients and use excerpts from these letters in his brochure. He also decided to print a company newsletter, the purpose of which would be to share with his customers some of the newer technological developments and product enhancements for both software and hardware. The newsletter would provide value to his customers in terms of valuable information, and it would provide value for Craig, as it would keep his name and the name of his company before his customers.

In other words, Craig developed a strategy to use the energy behind his anger constructively. Ruminating about the "unfair" awarding of the contract was a negative use of Craig's time and energy. Developing a proactive marketing strategy was a positive use of his time and energy.

Another way to use the concept of perspective management positively as a negotiator is to decide ahead of time what social role you want to take on as you negotiate. The theory of social roles as a form of self-control in the negotiation process is the next topic.

## The Power of Role Selection

We assume different roles all the time. In any given day you might play the role of a professional, a husband or wife, a parent, son or daughter, coach, Girl Scout leader, president of the PTA, and so on. When you assume each particular role, you take on certain characteristics of that role. For example, when my daughter suffered an eye accident while we were in a store, I saw my wife assume the role of physician, which is her occupation. Lynn calmly told the sales staff of the store to call the local children's hospital to alert them that we were bringing in a child whose eye had been severely traumatized. Lynn then calmly turned to me and asked if I thought I would be able to drive to the hospital. She remained calm throughout the trip, but as soon as Lynn turned our daughter over to the emergency room physician, she broke down. At that point, she allowed herself to leave the physician role and become Katie's mother.

When you can consciously choose what role you want to take during a negotiation, it gives you the power to select how you want to behave in that negotiation. It is important to look at times when you have used positive roles as frames to help you negotiate more effectively. For example, after my daughter's eye accident, I negotiated with the department store vice president regarding their safety standards. The vice president said, "As parents, we are all responsible for our children. As a parent, you are practically responsible for her accident." The parent in me wanted to throttle the man. However, in the negotiator/consumer advocate role, I was able to say, "If I had left my daughter unattended at an elevator or escalator, I could see how I would have been responsible; however, one would assume that one was in a relatively safe environment in the main aisle of your store. If you do not do everything in your power to protect the children who enter your store, I will have no other choice but to go to the press."

Take a moment now to think of at least one watershed moment when you were surprised at how well you maintained your self-control. Then complete the following Self-Control Form (Exercise 5.8) and identify the positive roles you have played (Exercise 5.9).

■  ■  ■  ■

## EXERCISE 5.8
### Self-Control Form

1.  Describe a negotiation in which you demonstrated excellent self-control.

What role were you playing in the above situation that helped you maintain good self-control?

2.  Describe another negotiation in which you demonstrated excellent self-control.

What role were you playing in the above situation that helped you maintain good self-control?

3.  Describe yet another negotiation in which you demonstrated excellent self-control.

What role were you playing in the above situation that helped you maintain good self-control?

■ ■ ■ ■

## EXERCISE 5.9
### Identification of Positive Roles

At this point, you have identified several situations in which you demonstrated excellent self-control in selected negotiations. You have also identified the "roles" you were playing in these negotiations that helped you maintain good self-control. In the space below, make a list of the positive "roles" that you can use on a more conscious and consistent basis to help you negotiate more effectively in the future:

■ ■ ■ ■

Just as it is important to be able to look at situations in which we can use positive roles as frames to help us negotiate more effectively, it is also important to look at situations in which we have inadvertently fallen into roles that prevent us from negotiating effectively. For example, at a workshop I was teaching for the government, one of the participants made a negative and unjustified comment against a particular group of citizens. I lost my cool, and called him on his remark in front of the other participants. I fell out of the "teacher/facilitator" role and into the role of "irate citizen." A more effective negotiator/teacher/facilitator would have addressed the matter in private with the person.

A colleague of mine states that she never loses her sense of calm as a negotiator in public, for she has developed an excellent "professional role" to help her be effective in her professional life. However, she says that she "loses it" too frequently in her home life, stating that it is easier for her to lose self-control with her family. She has chosen to keep a log at home to help her learn to be as effective a negotiator there as she is at work.

Exercise 5.10 asks you to briefly describe three incidents in which you did not demonstrate good self-control. After you have finished describing each situation, analyze it to determine how the role you played in each of the situations prevented you from maintaining your self-control (Exercise 5.11).

■   ■   ■   ■

### EXERCISE 5.10
### Improving Self-Control Form

1. Describe a negotiation in which you demonstrated poor self-control.

What role were you playing in the above situation that prevented you from maintaining good self-control?

2. Describe another negotiation in which you demonstrated poor self-control.

What role were you playing in the above situation that prevented you from maintaining good self-control?

3. Describe yet another negotiation in which you demonstrated poor self-control.

What role were you playing in the above situation that prevented you from maintaining good self-control?

■  ▓  ▓  ▓

## EXERCISE 5.11
## Identifying Negative Roles

At this point, you have identified several situations in which you were not able to demonstrate good self-control in selected negotiations. You have also identified the "roles" you were playing in these negotiations that prevented you from maintaining good self-control. In the space below, please list the negative "roles" that you played:

To negotiate more effectively in the future, you need to make a conscious effort not to fall into these roles.

▓  ▓  ▓  ▓

## The Power of Looking for Reasonable
## People in Unreasonable Situations

As part of my research for this book I interviewed effective negotiators, one of whom was Bill, who told me he learned a great deal about negotiation from his parents. One of these lessons was the phrase "In unreasonable situations, keep looking for reasonable people." I asked Bill if he could give me an example, and he told me the following story.

Bill's daughter Sarah was an honor student, which meant that all of her numerical grades were 90 and above in every subject—except for social studies, in which she received a 65. Sarah told her father that all the students in her class were complaining about their grades despite having tried hard.

Bill made an appointment to see the principal, hoping to get some advice on how Sarah could do better in the class. He also asked to see the class grade roster so that he could compare Sarah's grade in social studies with other grades in the class. The principal said that this was confidential information that could not be released. Bill stated that he did not want to see the students' names but only their grades so as to see the average in the social studies class. The principal stated that he could not do that and assured Bill that the social studies teacher was an excellent and accomplished instructor.

Bill stated again that he in no way wanted to violate confidentiality; he only wanted to see the numerical grades. If need be, Bill said, he would take his request to the superintendent of schools for the district. Then the principal covered the names and gave Bill a photocopied sheet that contained only the grades. These were compared with the averages for the same students in classes taught by several other teachers. Bill found that the average grade from the social studies class was 15 points lower than the average from the lowest of all the other classes.

Bill asked to look at the comments written by the social studies teacher concerning students' work and their progress in the class. None of the remarks were positive. All were negative.

It became apparent that Sarah's teacher might be the one with a problem. Bill asked to have a meeting with the principal, the social studies teacher, and Sarah's homeroom teacher. I asked him why he wanted the homeroom teacher present, and Bill said that Sarah was in two of her classes and knew Sarah well.

When Bill asked the social studies teacher to explain why the grades for his class averaged 15 points below all the other teachers' and why all the remarks he made about the students were negative, the teacher said that he had been having a tough year. To his credit, the teacher further explained that he was under severe emotional stress at home, and it was having an effect on his teaching. This teacher asked for and was granted a leave of absence for the remainder of the year.

■ ■ ■ ■

**EXERCISE 5.12**
**Case Study Analysis**

Name three things that Bill did well in this negotiation.

1.

2.

3.

Based on what you know about the above situation, is there anything you would do differently?

■ ■ ■ ■

### EXERCISE 5.13
### The Power of Looking for Reasonable People

In the space below, describe a situation in which you used the power of looking for reasonable people to bring about a positive outcome to a difficult situation:

■ ■ ■ ■

## The Power of Doing the Unexpected

When I was growing up in San Francisco, my grandmother and I frequently went exploring. One of my favorite places was Chinatown. It was on one of our trips to Chinatown that I discovered "the Chinese finger trap." This toy is a narrow tube made out of straw reeds. You insert a finger in one end and invite an unsuspecting friend to put a finger in the opposite end. Each person then tries to pull their finger out of the tube. The more you pull, the harder it is to get your finger out because pulling causes the tube to become narrower and tighter. The most common reaction is to pull harder, which only makes the tube tighter still. It is only when one person does the unexpected, pushing their finger into the tube instead of pulling out, that the tube becomes wide enough to release both fingers.

Often, it turns out that doing the unexpected helps disarm the "difficult person" with whom you are dealing. An example of this is apologizing to a belligerent customer who is expecting you to become belligerent in return. Jay Carter (1989), in his book titled *Nasty People: How to Stop Being Hurt by Them Without Becoming One of Them,* offers another example:

> A woman has been dominated by her husband for years. By passively condoning his domination, the wife has reinforced the very behavior she wants to change. In the latest round of negotiations, the wife wants to enroll in an evening course in psychology. The husband says, "If you take that course, I'll divorce you!" The wife's usual reply would have been to not take the course. This time, however, she replies, "I love you. I do not want a divorce; however, I am going to take this course because it interests me very much. If you want a divorce, you will have to file for it." In this case, the wife did the unexpected. She didn't take the bait, get hysterical, and say "How can you treat me this way?" Instead, she calmly told her husband that she loved him and did not want to get a divorce. She also told him that she was going to take the course and that if he wanted a divorce, it was his prerogative to file for one. (p. 26)

The "Change First Principle" states that if you want to change someone else's behavior or your relationship with that person, you have to change your own behavior first. In the literature on Brief Solution-Focused Therapy, this principle is stated as follows: "If it is working, do more of the same; if it isn't working, do something different."

"Doing the unexpected," the "Change First Principle," and "If it isn't working, do something different" all have a common element: changing a behavior pattern. When the old pattern no longer works, try a new pattern that does. To do this more frequently, you have to be aware of when we are at a "choice point"—those critical points in a negotiation in which, if you choose to do something different, the negotiation will move forward toward a settlement, whereas more of the same behavior will continue the old pattern, lead to breaking off the negotiation, or to an impasse, or the escalation of a fight.

These are such important concepts in negotiating they warrant one more example. I spend most of my time at work teaching people how to negotiate more effectively. My workshops are highly interactive, and the participants spend a lot of time doing simulations and role-plays. Just before the beginning of one workshop, one of the participants, Bob, came up to me and said, "I don't believe in role-playing. It is a complete waste of time. I have been to lots of workshops. I have never learned anything from doing it, and I refuse to do it in this workshop." (This made me a bit worried because my workshop is highly experiential and I have three to four negotiation role-play simulations in the two-day workshop.)

I replied that "there are some things that are difficult to learn any other way," to which Bob replied, "That's just a motherhood statement." (Obviously, I wasn't getting anywhere with this approach, so I changed strategies.)

I then said, "I am willing to be wrong." To my surprise, Bob replied, "I am willing to be wrong, too."

Bob went on to participant in every role-play in the course and even volunteered to do one of the most difficult ones in front of the entire class.

⬚ ⬚ ⬚ ⬚

### EXERCISE 5.14
### The Power of Doing the Unexpected

1. In the space below, describe a situation in which you used the power of the unexpected to help move a negotiation forward toward resolution.

⬚ ⬚ ⬚ ⬚

**The Power of Resiliency**

Even the best negotiators make mistakes. However, one of the factors that best differentiates effective negotiators from their less effective counterparts is the way they deal with their mistakes. Effective negotiators have more resiliency; they *accept* that they are human—not perfect— and they turn their mistakes into learning opportunities. Therefore, they have a shorter recovery time before returning to full effectiveness.

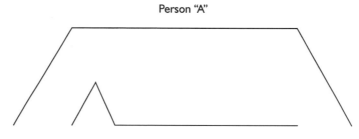

**Figure 5.1**    Shortening Recovery Time

One of the main components of resiliency as a negotiator is recovery time, which is the time that it takes a person to recover his or her equilibrium after a difficult negotiation. For example, we can beat ourselves up mentally for the next five minutes, five days, five months, or we can ask ourselves what we learned from the negotiation and/or specify what we would do differently if we were to renegotiate that same negotiation.

When you get mentally beaten up or emotionally hooked by a difficult person, or if you feel you have made an important mistake in a negotiation, you may lose control over the process and/or the outcome. There is, however, one thing that you do have absolute control over: the amount of time it takes you to recover.

Compare the graphs for person A and person B (Figure 5.1). We see that person A becomes more stressed and stays stressed longer than person B. There are several proven techniques that you can use to get yourself unhooked and to recover more quickly. Among the techniques previously covered in this chapter that can aid in recovery time are accurate diagnosis, understanding core values and core beliefs, effective anger management, and the power of keeping things in perspective.

When the above techniques have not worked, there is another approach you can take if you have become emotionally hooked: You can turn to outside help in the form of a good recovery coach. Good recovery coaches will tell you the truth as they see it, help you look at the situation from several perspectives, ask insightful questions to help you discover more effective alternatives, and offer analogies, metaphors, and stories from their experience to help you see alternatives. All of these will help you become a more effective negotiator.

For example, Tim developed a new marketing brochure for the company where he worked. He worked incredibly hard on this project and sent it to the company CEO for his comments. The CEO noted two minor problems with the presentation and then left for a meeting. Tim was devastated. His hours of work, dedication, and creativity were not acknowledged. Tim's motivation to work for the company went from extremely high to extremely low. It looked as though his recovery time to full effectiveness would take a long time. He talked about his problem with one of the company's managers, who helped Tim see that he had written a very good report and that the CEO was notorious for not acknowledging employees for their effort and accomplishments. In this case, talking to another manager reduced Tim's recovery time by 80%.

■ ■ ■ ■

### EXERCISE 5.15
### Shortening Recovery Time

1. Give an example of how talking to someone who acted in the role of a recovery coach helped shorten your recovery time:

2. Effective negotiators have at least four people with whom they can talk who are very effective in helping them learn from their mistakes and reduce their recovery time. In the space below, list four people you can turn to who can help you learn from your mistakes and reduce your recovery time:

■ ■ ■ ■

# Developing Higher-Order Skills

Mastery of most skills depends on an accurate analysis and on dedicated practice—both are necessary, neither alone is sufficient.

■ ■ ■ ■

This chapter discusses higher-order negotiating skills and subskills and how to develop them using the "P.R.I.C.E." method. Also explored is the value of learning by interviewing experienced negotiators and learning from mentors. As negotiating and influencing skills must work together congruently and harmoniously to be truly effective, the chapter provides five techniques for putting all your skills together into an effective, integrated whole.

## ▩ Higher-Order Skills

One of the psychological concepts that has had the most impact on my way of thinking about how adults learn is that of *higher-order skills,* an idea developed by Francis Robinson, a psychologist. In explaining this concept, Robinson used the analogy of learning to swim for pleasure versus preparing to swim in the Olympics. In the latter case, the person is developing higher-order swimming skills—that is, skills "based on scientific research on how to reduce the resistance of the body in the water and on how to obtain the most powerful forward push with the least effort" (Robinson, 1970, p.11).

Let us assume that our swimmer will be competing in the 100-meter freestyle and that she has just been assigned a new coach. One of the first things her coach does is perform a "differential diagnosis," which here entails asking our athlete to swim the full length of the pool using her arms only, then to swim the same distance using only her legs to propel herself through the water, and finally to swim the length of the pool using both her arms and legs.

What is the coach doing? He is looking at the relative contribution of the upper body and the lower body to the total effort. In most cases, the average swimmer kicks to remain horizontal in the water. Olympic swimmers derive at minimum 6% of their forward motion from their kick. By careful measurement, the coach in this example determines that our athlete is only achieving a 4% forward thrust from her kick.

The differential diagnosis has made it clear that this is a major part of our swimmer's stroke that needs work. Each of us needs to know which skills are working well and which skills are most in need of improvement, for we are only as good as the weakest link. It is the same in improving negotiating skills—you must do an accurate differential diagnosis and improve your weaker skills.

It is important to note that the idea of higher-order skills includes making improvements not only in areas where one is weak but also continuing to improve in areas where one's skills are strong. For example, let's suppose that you are an excellent listener but need improvement in self-control while dealing with people who appear to be rigid. Most people would assume that one would make the most gains by learning one or several of the self-control techniques, such as perspective management. However, you might make an equally profound impact on your negotiating skills by improving your already excellent listening skills. Two things are very valuable about the idea of developing higher-order skills. First, it is a technology that works. Second, it reminds you that there is no ceiling on your already well-developed skills.

At this point, we need to return to our swimming analogy to illustrate the concept of salient feedback. Let's assume that our athlete has worked exceedingly hard both in the pool and on dry land to develop strength in her lower body, which has resulted in an additional 6% increase in her forward motion. This together with upper-body strength building and improvements in her technique have placed her among the top ten 100-meter freestyle swimmers in the world. However, she has yet to rank higher than a fifth-place finish, well outside contention for a medal. Her coach completes another differential diagnosis, which shows that the front-arm extension of her stroke into the water needs to be a fraction of a millimeter longer as does the follow-through extension at the end of her stroke.

Although our swimmer understands this concept and has seen it demonstrated by her coach and other world-class swimmers, she just can't seem to do it. The coach then decides to videotape our swimmer. Using the VCR's freeze-frame and slow-motion features, he is able to show her exactly where her arms enter and leave the water as opposed to the place where her arms ought to enter and leave the water. Seeing her stroke on the television monitor acts as salient feedback, which has had so much impact on our swimmer that she changed her stroke and is now in contention for an Olympic medal.

There are three important elements in developing higher-order skills:

- An accurate differential diagnosis of the relative strengths of the skills that make up the whole
- Salient feedback that is so accurate and personally meaningful that it helps change one's behavior in the desired direction
- Contined development of one's best skills with no artificial ceilings set

The following section describes one technique—the P.R.I.C.E. method—that can help you develop higher-order negotiating and influencing skills.

## ▒ The P.R.I.C.E. Method

Most of us achieve a certain skill level and then become complacent and rest unnecessarily at that level. Increasing proficiency requires the removal of these psychological blinders and advancing to higher-order skills. To develop such skills and to bring about an increase in their effectiveness, you must "pay the P.R.I.C.E.," which stands for *P*inpoint, *R*ecord, *I*ntervene, *C*oach, and *E*valuate.

### Pinpoint

Pinpointing is the establishment of specific, concrete, positive change goals. Psychologists call these goals "target behaviors."

Most people think they are being specific when, in fact, they are being vague. You know your target behavior is specific when the behavior is defined in observable and measurable terms. For example, the phrase "poor morale" is not specific. Do you mean that people are coming to work late? Or that the quality of the work is poor? Or that people are bickering at work? You know when you are being specific enough when the behavior you are trying to define passes the "yes/no" test. The "yes/no" test states that the behavior has to be defined specifically enough that through observation you can say that "yes" it did occur or "no" it did not occur. For example, when I found myself getting really annoyed with the person I was negotiating with, "yes" I took a break from the table and planned my strategy by using one or more muscle levels, or "no" I did not take a break from the table nor use any muscle level.

Put the *emphasis on positive behaviors* (e.g., spending more time doing bookkeeping for my business and less time watching TV). Changing your own or someone else's behavior is *always* more effective when the emphasis is on the positive behavior you would like to see occur. People have trouble admitting there are problems, but nearly everyone can accept the idea of improving themselves. Sometimes, however, you may want to record both positive and negative events—that is, target those instances when you kept your self-control while being provoked and those when you lost your self-control while being provoked. You can then perform a differential diagnosis to determine the key factors that differentiated between your keeping and losing self-control.

Good psychologists, managers, supervisors, parents, teachers, and coaches use shaping when identifying target behaviors: They start at a low enough level to ensure success and increase performance in small, easily achieved steps. For example, goal attainment scaling suggests having at least five progressive performance levels.

### Record

Recording behavior is a strong intervention on its own. Each of us is a much poorer observer than we think we are. To improve your powers of observation, you need to observe systematically. In doing so, you obtain valuable information that will help you develop a viable self-change project.

Recording forces you to establish areas to be measured and ways to measure them—for example, by quantity, quality, cost (on or off budget and by how much), or in terms of time.

Recording is such a powerful technique that just by recording the behavior, that behavior is very likely to change. This is known as "O. Linsley's Law."

### Intervene

By analyzing your observations, you can draw conclusions about the problem and generate possible solutions. You are then in a much better position to develop a workable self-change plan.

Your intervention should be set up for a three-week period. Any shorter time period does not allow enough time to "get the bugs out" or for the behavior to become habitual. Any longer time period makes it difficult to stay focused while waiting for the results. After successfully completing your initial three-week project, you can then commit to a second, longer time period.

### Coach

Coaching can mean self-coaching or asking someone to serve as your coach for the duration of your self-change project. Coaching essentially means asking someone to observe your performance and give you feedback on results. This process is set up ahead of time by agreement with your coach, including when and how the coach will give you feedback. By using an external feedback system, you increase the chances of accomplishing your goals.

Feedback should be as immediate as possible. If the feedback is vague and/or delayed, it is not as effective. Use numbers whenever possible. You may have achieved your goal 100%. You bettered your goal by 1, or you missed your goal by a factor of 10. Once the goal is set, feedback should relate specifically to that goal.

## Evaluate

At the end of the three-week time period, evaluate the results of your self-change project. Do you want to maintain your progress? If yes, how will you ensure that you do? Is there another self-change project you would like to try? Is there someone else you would like to work with on a self-change project? Remember to KISS: *Keep It Short and Simple.* If you have too many projects going on at once or if the steps are too big or the project too complex, it won't work!

## P.R.I.C.E. in Action

Here are some examples of how my workshop participants used each of the elements of the P.R.I.C.E. method to develop specific aspects of their negotiating skills.

### Example 1

Anthony works in the zone office for one of the large automobile manufacturing companies. Zone offices act as the manufacturer's representative in various regions of the country. Anthony's job is to look into customer complaints, so the people he deals with are usually not happy because they have not been able to get their complaint resolved to their satisfaction by the dealership where they bought their cars. To resolve the problem, Anthony not only has to negotiate with the customer and the local dealership but also sometimes with the national office. He also plays the role of mediator between the parties and sometimes must negotiate the customer's acceptance that the responsibility for the problem lies with neither the manufacturer nor the dealership. As you can imagine, this can be a difficult and stressful job.

Anthony's company sent him to a professional development course on effective customer service. A major component of the course was "active listening." Although Anthony had heard about active listening many times before, this particular course used the P.R.I.C.E. system to make sure that the learning which took place actually transferred to the work environment.

Anthony wanted to use active listening skills to do a better job in responding to customer complaints. However, understanding the technique and knowing how to make it a part of everyday behavior are two different matters. This is where pinpointing comes into place.

Anthony knew that customers need to feel that their complaints are understood, even if their diagnosis of the problem is incorrect. In using active listening, Anthony decided that it would be helpful to paraphrase or restate a customer's complaint by using intermediate summaries to summarize the situation for the customer at appropriate times throughout the telephone call.

The cue he used to remind himself to give periodic summaries was a happy face placed next to the telephone (intervention). The happy face served as a reminder that the purpose of his job was to satisfy the customer. He also decided to keep his daytimer next to the telephone, open to the current date. Every time Anthony used an intermediate summary while answering a consumer complaint, he marked it in his daytimer (recording).

As you can see from the graph in Figure 6.1 (evaluating), by using the techniques of cueing and recording, Anthony increased his use of intermediate summaries by 80% during the three-week trial period. By the end of the third week, giving intermediate summaries became a natural part of Anthony's on-the-job behavior. As a side benefit, Anthony told me his wife was pleased because she felt that he was communicating more effectively at home.

As you can see from this example, not every element from the P.R.I.C.E. system was necessary in this intervention. This was purely a self-monitoring project, which eliminated the need for coaching. The following example demonstrates a situation in which all the P.R.I.C.E. elements were necessary to bring about the desired changes:

▓ Example 2

Natalie works in the public relations department of a large manufacturing company. The department has recently undergone restructuring, and Natalie now reports to Claire, the new department head. Previous to this arrangement, Claire and Natalie were coworkers. Their relationship looked cordial enough on the surface, but in truth they were extremely competitive.

This competitiveness has carried over into their new working relationship, the major difference being that now Natalie reports to Claire. The

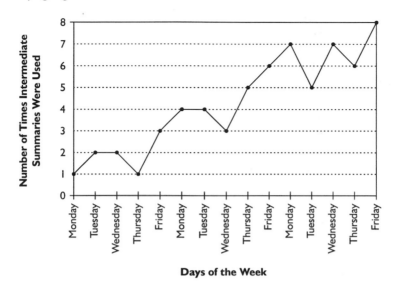

**Figure 6.1** Anthony's Graph of Progress Over Time

tension between them has increased, and Natalie is beginning to feel inse-cure about her job. In the past, she received constant praise from her ex-boss. Now, instead of praise she receives a constant barrage of criticism from Claire. Natalie feels her motivation and self-esteem slipping. At present, there are no other job openings in public relations in her city. She feels trapped in a bad situation.

Natalie makes an appointment to see Ken, who had been her supervisor 12 years ago and with whom Natalie had a mentoring relationship. Ken suggests that they use the P.R.I.C.E. method to see if the situation is changeable.

*Pinpoint.* Under pinpoint, Natalie suggests that she does not want to receive so much negative feedback. Ken asks her to translate her request into a positive target behavior. Natalie is then able to say that she wants to receive some positive feedback from Claire. Ken responds by suggesting that she monitor the incidence of positive feedback.

*Record.* They decide to note all instances of positive feedback in Natalie's daytimer with a tally next to the half-hour segment in which the positive feedback occurs. Natalie is to record as specifically as possible the wording of the positive feedback, which will give her some sense of both the quality and the quantity of the feedback.

*Intervene.* They decide that during the first week of the time period there will be no formal intervention. This is a time to sample the behavior as it is occurring in the environment. Psychologists call this "collecting baseline data."

*Coach.* This segment is fulfilled by the meetings between Ken and Natalie in which Ken acts as coach.

*Evaluate.* As shown in the first week of baseline data, there are three instances of positive feedback:

- "You did a good job on the newsletter for the Smith account."
- "I think Fred will like the new layout for his newsletter."
- "I like the colors you chose for the computer ad."

Natalie is amazed. Without having these data, she would swear that she doesn't get any positive feedback. What she is able to determine with the P.R.I.C.E method is that, yes, she does get some positive reinforcement. The ratio of negative to positive reinforcement has been so high that she hasn't noticed having received any positive feedback at all. The next time she meets with Ken, he asks her about the quality of the feedback. They determine that some of the feedback is vague (e.g., "You did a good job on the newsletter for the Smith account"), but some is more specific (e.g., "I like the colors you chose for the computer ad").

Ken then helps Natalie design a new intervention for the following week. When Claire gives negative feedback, Natalie is to ask specifically what changes will make the assignment acceptable the next time. When the positive feedback is vague (e.g., "You did a good job"), Natalie is to ask for specifics (e.g., "Please tell me what made it good, so I will know what to do next time").

As you can see from the graph in Figure 6.2, the quantity of positive feedback increased substantially over the subsequent three-week period.

### Putting It All Together: The Whole Is Not Equal to the Sum of Its Parts

If you are to be a truly effective negotiator, all your negotiating skills must work together congruently and harmoniously. It is one of the most

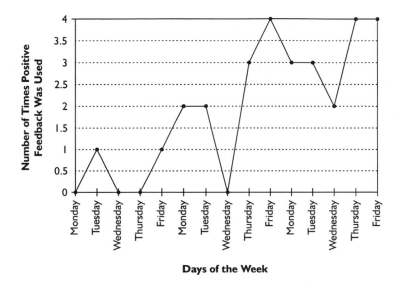

**Figure 6.2**  Claire's Graph of Progress Over Time

difficult aspects of learning how to negotiate effectively. This section describes four techniques for putting these skills together to form an effective, unified whole:

- Congruence
- Skills becoming second nature
- Using two seemingly paradoxical elements in the negotiating process simultaneously
- Harvard's training in IPS (interpersonal skills)

### Congruence

As stated in Chapter 1, negotiating is like a symphony orchestra of skills. All the skills have to work together congruently and harmoniously. If even one player in the orchestra is less than fully developed as a musician, the symphony will not sound as good as it should. Likewise, if even one of your negotiating skills is less than fully developed, you will not negotiate as well as you otherwise could.

If one member of the orchestra is playing a different tune, or even the right tune at the wrong place in the symphony, the music will not sound as good as it could or should. Likewise, if you are using the wrong skill, or even the right skill at the wrong time, your negotiation will not go as well as it could or should.

Leonard Bernstein (1959) captured this sense of congruence exceedingly well in his book *The Joy of Music*. In the fifth chapter, which is about Beethoven's Fifth Symphony, Bernstein recounts a telecast that took place on November 14, 1954, the text of which is reproduced here:

> We are going to try to perform for you today a curious and rather difficult experiment. We're going to take the first movement of Beethoven's *Fifth Symphony* and rewrite it. Now don't get scared; we're going to use only notes that Beethoven himself wrote. We're going to take certain discarded sketches that Beethoven wrote, intending to use them in this symphony, and find out why he rejected them, by putting them back into the symphony and seeing how the symphony would have sounded with them. Then we can guess at the reason for rejecting these sketches, and what is more important, perhaps we can get a glimpse into the composer's mind as it moves through this mysterious creative process we call composing.
>
> We have here painted on the floor a reproduction of the first page of the conductor's score for Beethoven's *Fifth Symphony*. Every time I look at this orchestral score I am amazed all over again at its simplicity, strength and rightness. And how economical the music is! Why, almost every bar of this first movement is a direct development of these opening four notes.
>
> And what are these notes that they should be so pregnant and meaningful that a whole symphonic movement can be born of them? Three G's and an E-flat. Nothing more. [Nothing less] . . . (pp. 73-74)

What does this tell us about effective negotiating? Two things, at least. A perfect symphony is like a perfect negotiation. Everything that is in it needs to be there. Also, nothing is in it that does not need to be there. There is a harmony and congruence between the parts and the whole. Bernstein also speaks eloquently about the simplicity, strength, and rightness of the opening notes. Good negotiators know how important simplicity, strength, and rightness are in their opening statement. In the symphony, the opening tends to set the tone for the entire symphony that follows. In negotiating, the opening statement tends to set the tone for the entire negotiation that follows. The simplicity, strength, and rightness of your opening statement will have a lot to do with the tone, process, and outcome of your negotiation.

## Skills Becoming Second Nature

Expert negotiators become so proficient at certain skills in the negotiating process that they do not have to consciously think about using those skills. It's as if the response becomes second nature. For example, Diane stated that she practiced the "Getting to Yes" model so frequently that there are parts of the model that she no longer has to think about. In particular, the part of the model that suggests using external criteria to help resolve problems, disputes, and conflicts has become second nature to her. Diane states, "Before I even realize it, I have referred to some sort of external objective criteria to help resolve the problem." She reports that not only does she make extensive use of external criteria in her own negotiation, she also uses external criteria frequently to help friends and colleagues when they ask for her advice in their negotiations.

You will know that you are making progress as a negotiator when your skills start to become second nature. You will then be free to think about other elements in the process. You will also know that you are making progress in the negotiating process when you are able to use two seemingly paradoxical elements simultaneously. This is the next step in becoming a truly proficient negotiator.

## Using Two Seemingly Paradoxical Elements in the Negotiating Process Simultaneously

You are well on your way to developing higher-order negotiating skills when you can actively listen and be assertive simultaneously. In most cases, you have to listen actively first to find out the other party's interests; you have to step to the other party's side. Then you can be assertive and explain your interests.

When I speak of listening actively and being assertive simultaneously, I mean that you must also listen carefully to the way the other party "frames" their arguments, for it tells you a great deal about the interests behind their interests. You can then use their "frame" to present your interests. By using their "frame," it is much more likely that the other party will be able to "hear" and "accept" your reasoning.

This technique is complex and difficult to learn. It is not usually something that can be grasped at once; you have to keep working on it. It is also one of the most powerful of the negotiating strategies, so it is well worth the time and effort to learn it.

I am often asked, "Isn't this a form of manipulation?" Unfortunately, the word itself invokes negative or even sinister connotations; yet everyone use frames all the time to be more persuasive. The challenge is to be persuasive and to be open to being persuaded by others. As an effective negotiator, you need to be able to do both simultaneously.

Let's look at a specific example. John and his son Tony were visiting a friend in Fairfax, California. The friend's home was high up in the hills overlooking the town. At the time of the visit, John's son Tony was 6 years old and his friend's son Matthew was 4. John offered to walk the two boys into town so they could play on the local playground. The boys enthusiastically said yes.

John asked the boys if they needed to use the washroom, and of course, both boys said no. The threesome started walking down the long road to the town. A half hour later, when they arrived at the outskirts of town, Tony said he had to "go poo really badly." Luckily, they were just across the street from one of the town's two gas stations. Unluckily, it had run out of toilet paper.

They quickly walked to the town's other gas station, two blocks away. When they got there and asked for the restroom key, they were told that the restrooms were for customers only. John appealed to the man, saying that his son needed to use the facilities. The man looked back impassively and stated, "It's company policy; only customers can use the facility."

By listening carefully, John heard the attendant's "frame": "Only customers can use the facility." John then knew he had to reframe his situation. The frame of being a stranger in town in need of help, although persuasive to many other people, was not at all persuasive for this particular attendant. By listening carefully, however, he heard that the frame "being a customer" probably would be persuasive. John then purchased two bags of potato chips for the boys and asked the attendant if that made him a customer. His request to use the restroom was granted.

Note that John did not persist with the frame of being a stranger in need; he did not appeal to the attendant's experience with children, nor did he try to get the attendant to sympathize with the child's need. He carefully listened to the attendant's frame and then used it to help him realize his own interests within the attendant's frame of reference.

■ ■ ■ ■

## EXERCISE 6.1
### Identifying Frames

Describe a situation in which you used another person's "frame" successfully to help further your own interests.

■ ■ ■ ■

## EXERCISE 6.2
### Using Frames to Persuade

Can you think of a current situation in which you need to do a better job of using the power of active listening? By using the other party's frame, how might you reframe that particular situation to increase the likelihood that the other party will be able to see a solution to your mutual interests within his or her reframed perspective?

■ ■ ■ ■

■  The Power of Empathy

Roger Fisher, director of the Harvard Program on Negotiation, states that you cannot change someone's mind about an issue unless you first know their thoughts and feelings about it.

The more difficulty you are having with another person, the more likely you are to accentuate the differences between you, and the less likely you are to be empathetic. For this reason, it is especially important to make a conscious effort to understand the other party. Role reversal is an excellent tool to help you better understand the person with whom you are negotiating.

## Role Reversal

Role reversal is a very effective method to help you understand the other person's point of view. In this exercise, you play the role of the other person in the negotiation, and a friend plays your role. To prepare for this, you must coach your friend to accurately play your role. You will learn a great deal from this exercise in two important ways: First, by actively role-playing the other party, you gain insight into the way he or she sees the world both on an intellectual level and on an emotional level. Second, by watching someone else play your role, you gain insight into where your skills and strategies work and where they need to improve.

For example, in my advanced negotiation workshops, I ask the participants to get together in groups of 3 and to write down and share a negotiation that they had been involved in that didn't go as well as they would have liked and/or that was with someone with whom they had difficulty communicating. The person whose case it is then plays the role of the difficult person, the second group member plays the role of the participant in the original negotiation, and the third group member plays the role of coach/observer.

At one workshop, a participant named Ross shared a story about negotiating with a difficult person. Ross was sure that his case was unresolvable because the organization for whom he worked had developed a new scheduling system that Ross was supposed to enforce but which relied on the goodwill of his staff. One of Ross's supervisees, Tim, was a staunch "union" person who refused to change to the new schedule.

Although it was true that Ross could not force his subordinate to try the new system, after playing the role of his "recalcitrant subordinate" and with the help of his coach, Ross was able to see how he could bargain for Tim's cooperation. By playing Tim's role, Ross was able to gain some very valuable insight into Tim's motivation and subsequently convince him to change hours. The new scheduling system allowed Tim to run for the union executive position, which he had always wanted to do. Ross reports that he never would have thought of this solution without the role-reversal exercise. Role reversal is an excellent technique for testing your assumptions and for ensuring that you are as well prepared as you can be for important negotiations.

## Harvard's Training in IPS (Interpersonal Skills)

One of the best methods I have seen to help people prepare themselves for difficult negotiations is IPS, an exercise developed at Harvard Law School to take the power of role-playing several steps further. You can use it to increase your own learning. This exercise has eight steps:

- Enrolling
- Identifying skill(s)
- Doubling
- Baseline take(s)
- Overshoot
- Ideal take(s)
- Debriefing
- Following through

The exercise works best with groups of 3 participants. If videotaping is done, the camera operator is counted as a fourth person. As this is a complicated process, each of these eight steps is described below.

### Enrolling

Each person in the group is asked to prepare a written description of a difficult person, situation, or conversation. This can be a situation that has already occurred, one that is ongoing, or one that the participant anticipates will occur in the near future. Each participant is asked to prepare a sample dialogue of the difficult conversation. An example of a problem situation and the accompanying dialogue of the difficult conversation is reproduced in Figure 6.3. Note that the dialogue includes a section on what you thought and felt during each segment of the conversation.

Writing a description of the problem situation and the accompanying dialogue provides insight that will help you negotiate better in the future.

| **What I Felt or Thought** | **What the Participants Said** |
| --- | --- |
| I would like to get this resolved nonadversarially. | Brad: I would like to get the work finished on our cottage. |
| I feel badly that you have been sick—and I see you working for other people. | Doug: I've been sick. I'll have to get to it later. |
| Two years is a long time. We have been very patient. | Brad: It's been two years. Can you give me a specific date? |
| This guy is hard to pin down. What's wrong with him? | Doug: I'll try to get to it in the next two weeks, but I have a lot to do so I can't promise. |
| I'm getting very angry. | Brad: I think we have been very patient. |
| That's not true!! | Doug: Sometimes, the smallest things can take the most time. Besides, it's a freebie, anyway. |

**Figure 6.3**

The description and the dialogue also helps the person playing "the other party" understand his or her part in the role-play. Use the blank form in Exercise 6.4 to try this technique.


▨ ▨ ▨ ▨

**EXERCISE 6.3**
**Writing a Sample Dialogue**

| **What I Felt or Thought** | **What the Participants Said** |
| --- | --- |
| | |

▨ ▨ ▨ ▨

In the first role-play, the participant who is working on his or her negotiating skills plays the role of the "difficult person." The second person plays the working participant's role, and the third person takes the role of the observer. The purpose of this role-play is to help each person better understand the dynamics of this particular negotiation. After the role-play, make sure you have 10 to 20 minutes to debrief. During the debriefing segment, people can ask for clarification, the dynamics can be discussed, and the observer and the others can make helpful comments.

### Identifying Skills

This is a crucial part of the exercise, for here the participants choose the skills they want to learn—but, note, at an appropriate level of difficulty. One of the most common mistakes is to choose too difficult a skill or too many skills or to attempt a combination of skills before one is ready.

At the advanced level, participants have an opportunity to work on advanced skills and/or combinations of skills. As an example of combined skills, one participant stated that he wanted to be more nonadversarially assertive and, at the same time, do a better job of listening actively to understand the underlying concerns of the other party and help the other person better understand his own underlying concerns and interests. This participant also wanted to keep his voice calm and relaxed while speaking slowly and distinctly and without tension in his voice. Even though this person is an experienced negotiator and has had a great deal of training in negotiation skills, I thought that he was attempting to do too much. I was wrong. This combination of goals was at exactly the right level for him. Although the skills set he sought was a reach from where he was, it was not so far as to make the task impossible. In the end, he reached his goals.

Regarding goals identification, there are two major mistakes that participants make: The first is to pick too difficult a goal and the second is to pick a goal that is not difficult enough.

### Doubling

The purpose of this part of the exercise is to help the person playing the "other party" learn to take on that role. This technique was originally devised to help actors develop a better sense of the person whose role they will be playing. In the first stage of doubling, the "other party" sits in a chair and describes the situation from his or her point of view. The participant whose case it is sits behind and to one side of the "other party." If the other party makes any mistakes in describing the situation, the party whose case it is corrects the facts and the underlying assumptions and then comments on the way the "other party" delivers his or her lines so that person will be as much like the "problem" person as possible.

### ▓ Baseline Take

During the baseline take, the "other party" plays the role of the difficult person. You play yourself in the negotiation, and the observer observes. It may be necessary to do several "takes" of this negotiation until everyone has their roles just right and the simulation becomes as close as possible to the original situation.

### ▓ Overshoot

When you learn a new skill or try to take a new skill to a higher level, you often are required to move out of your comfort zone, which tempts you to inhibit yourself. The element of "overshoot" was added to help break down your inhibitions and stretch your comfort zone by providing a safe environment in which to experiment. Perhaps the best way to explain the concept of overshoot is with the following example:

A major component of the skill set I wanted to learn was to be more nonadversarial. During the overshoot, I was asked to be aggressive. The experience was both fun and cathartic. For one of the people in my triad, the overshoot was to be condescending to someone who was being condescending to him. Ralph was aided in this by being asked to stand on a chair and look down on the person playing the role of being condescending to him. The third person in my group was having difficulty because it was easy for her to get hooked (she was a very caring person) by emotionally needy people. Part of the overshoot for Judy was to stand at the opposite end of the room from the person who was asking for an unreasonable amount of help. In this case, the physical distance between the two participants came to act as a metaphor for the emotional distance that Judy needed to keep between herself and overly needy people.

▧   Ideal Take

The purpose of the ideal take is to give the participant as many chances as needed to demonstrate the skill or skills set that he or she is trying to master.

▧   Debriefing

The observer's job is to act as a coach. All the observers can give valuable feedback to those trying to improve their skill level. Also, "overshoot" and/or "ideal take" can be tape-recorded and played back to the participants as a form of salient feedback. The tapes showing "baseline," "overshoot," and "ideal take" can be given to the participants to reinforce what they have learned.

▧   Following Through

Using the P.R.I.C.E. method, the buddy system, and/or reviewing tape recordings can help ensure that the new skill is maintained.

## ▧   Integrating the Lessons Learned

As stated at the beginning of this book, negotiating skills are like a symphony orchestra. To produce a harmonious and seamless piece of music, all the parts have to work together congruently. The same can be said of negotiating and influencing: All your skills must work together congruently if you are to negotiate effectively across an increasingly large number of situations and with diverse types of people.

▧   ▧   ▧   ▧

### EXERCISE 6.4
### Integrating Skills

In the space below, pick two skills that you would like to work on simultaneously—for example, active listening and assertiveness, creating value and claiming value, or being persuasive and being open to persuasion. Then develop a plan using the P.R.I.C.E. method or any other method to help ensure that you accomplish this very important and very difficult task.

▩ ▩ ▩ ▩

It is now time to examine what you have learned on a more "macro" level. In Exercise 6.5, you are asked to integrate what you have learned about negotiating from reading this book, from the feedback you have received from doing the exercises in this book, from feedback you have obtained from other people about how you negotiate effectively and about what you need to do to improve, and from your observations of other negotiators.

▩ ▩ ▩ ▩

## EXERCISE 6.5
### My New Approach

Write a brief memo (three to four paragraphs) to yourself, outlining your new approach to negotiating.

▩ ▩ ▩ ▩

ne suggestion that has worked very well for the participants in my training urses is to examine this statement at preset intervals, such as the end of ch month. At that time, you may change, revise, or update your memo. oing over the memo on a monthly basis with a peer mentor or a peer-entoring group can also be very helpful.

# The Power of Commitment

■ ■ ■ ■

This chapter explores the power of commitment in the negotiating process by examining a long-term contentious negotiation from start to finish. This negotiation involved building coalitions, increasing muscle level, and applying the power of using objective criteria and external standards. Techniques and strategies are discussed as the case study unfolds—a negotiation to improve display safety in stores after my daughter sustained a serious eye accident.

To help you develop an in-depth understanding of the negotiation process that occurred, much of the story is told through letters written by the concerned parties. To help you further develop your understanding of the "Getting to Yes" model, commentary is offered on why we did what we did.

## ■ The Case Study

On November 9, 1991, my wife and I were shopping in the children's shoe section at "National" Department Store with our two children, Andrew, age 4, and Katie, 18 months. Katie was attracted by a display of character slippers, which to her looked like stuffed animals. She ran over to play with the slippers and, as toddlers do, tripped and fell face first into the display. It happened so quickly that I was not able to catch her. I watched horrified, for I saw that the character slippers were displayed on hooks (one-quarter inch in diameter and eight inches long) projecting from a pegboard. A hook had caught Katie in the eye. At first I thought that she had impaled her eye on the hook. I screamed for my wife, who is a physician. As Lynn examined Katie, I asked her if it was bad, and she said that the hook had lacerated the eye. Horrified, we immediately left for the children's hospital.

Upon arrival at the emergency room, Katie was screaming with pain and bleeding from a very swollen left eye. She was seen by the staff pediatrician as a top priority, and Ophthalmology was consulted. Katie's vision was assessed as intact, but further examination was required. X rays were taken to rule out any fracture of the bone between the eye and the nose—for Katie, a terrifying experience, as both her parents had to forcibly restrain her.

The ophthalmologist told us that a full assessment of the eye would require examination under anesthetic, followed by a two-hour recovery period. The examination showed that Katie had a laceration of both the upper eyelid and of the conjunctiva (white of the eye). The conjunctival laceration was less than one-sixteenth of an inch from her cornea. There was no bleeding internally, and the laceration was through the top layer of the eyeball only. She and we appeared to be very lucky.

The entire procedure from accident to our return home took six-and-one-half hours. The trauma to Katie and ourselves was agonizing. She continued to be fearful and woke crying for several days after the accident.

The accident could have been far more serious than it was, and it did not need to happen. In view of the obvious potential risk carried by this type of pegboard display, we asked National to eliminate such displays from child height throughout its chain of stores. We stated that we thought it appropriate that large retailers such as National be leaders regarding the safety of their customers, particularly of those least able to protect themselves—namely, children.

We spoke with the local store manager and were told that the issue would be addressed at the local, regional, and national levels. We requested that the store keep us informed.

As the swelling went down and the eye patch came off, we found out that we were not so lucky. Katie frequently fell down, had started holding her head to the right, and could not pick objects up off the floor. We went back to the children's hospital, and after further examination were told that there had been some neurological and/or muscular damage caused by the hook pushing the eye back into the orbit. We were also told that there was a 90% chance that the condition would correct itself. If there were no change in six months, corrective surgery would be considered. We conveyed this information to National in the following letter:

*December 4, 1991*

Mr. Smith
Vice President of Operations
"National" Department Store

Dear Mr. Smith:

Unfortunately, since our letter to you of November 12, 1991, we have learned that our daughter, Katie McRae, has sustained neurological damage resulting from the accident at your store. The fourth cranial nerve to the left eye was damaged, leaving her with paralysis of the extraocular muscle called superior oblique. This means that her eye is involuntarily turned upward and, in fact, she is completely unable to pull her gaze down. The result is that her eyes are no longer aligned and she is left with double vision. The only way she can compensate for this is to hold her head tilting down and to the right.

It is our hope that the nerve will regenerate itself. If it has not done so within six months, our daughter will probably require surgery to correct the problem and be exposed to all the attendant risks.

Interim complications which may occur include amblyopia, a condition in which a child compensates for double vision by actually seeing with only one eye at a time. If this becomes permanent, depth perception is lost. This is a serious impairment which interferes with a number of activities, particularly driving. The constant tipping of the head to one side can cause shortening of the sternocleidomastoid muscle, which can cause neck problems. Katie also is at risk of further injury, as she is more prone to tripping over things which she sees as double. Her gait and level of activity have been altered, which could have far-reaching effects. There have been stresses placed on the whole family by this injury, ranging from specialist appointments to worry and preoccupation on the part of the parents.

In short, this accident can no longer be seen as a minor incident with no sequelae.

With concern,

Brad McRae
Lynn Crosby, MD

I should state that our first priority was that Katie's eyesight return to normal. Our second priority was that everything be done to prevent this type of accident from occurring in the future.

It seems that our letters had crossed in the mail. In early December, we received Mr. Smith's response to our first letter. His letter appears below:

*November 28, 1991*

Dear Drs. McRae and Crosby,

I am most appreciative of your letter and since I have received same I have had a look at a number of our stores and clearly we have kiddy hazards.

We are talking now to our display and fixture vendors in regard to a suitable cap.

Further, when we take our post-Christmas inventory, we will address the location of pegboard hooks.

I will keep you posted on our progress. I enclose two of our Charity Bears, one for Andrew and one for Katie.

Compliments of the Season to you all,

Yours sincerely,

John Smith
Vice President of Operations

I was livid after reading Smith's letter. First, our child came very close to losing an eye in his store, and he talked of "kiddy hazards"! She is a child, not a kid, and we are talking about the potential of a very serious and debilitating injury, not "hazards." Second, Smith proposed end caps to cover the display hooks, and end caps do nothing to prevent "blunt" eye injury. Third, he talked about addressing the location of pegboard hooks after Christmas, when Christmas is the time when the store is most heavily frequented by children. I found his response to Katie's accident and the potential for future accidents unconscionable.

At this point, I was too angry to negotiate further. I knew I had to "go to the balcony" to regain my perspective and to refocus on the desired outcome. The number one priority was that Katie's eyesight would recover. For this we had to wait because we had no direct control over the outcome. Our second priority was that display safety be improved for everyone (i.e., for children and adults) and not only in National's chain but in all retail stores in Canada. Once I was able to step back, get myself untangled emotionally, regain my perspective, and look at the larger picture, I was ready to begin negotiating again.

It appeared to us that the store wasn't taking our concerns seriously enough. We needed to be in a stronger negotiating position. One way to do this was to do a more thorough job of researching and preparing our case.

We approached the local children's hospital to determine whether it had any records of similar types of display-hook-related injuries. The hospital referred us to the Bureau of Chronic Disease Epidemiology's Laboratory Center for Disease Control, which has a database on all injuries reported to the emergency department at children's hospitals across Canada. A search of the database, which contained 85,000 records at the time, showed 19 records of injuries associated with displays in public places within the past 18 months, which was as long as the Bureau had been keeping records. More specifically, the research data showed that

> among the 19 records, six were associated with hooks on pegboards. Three of the injuries involved four-year-old children, two involved three-year-olds and one involved a one-year-old. All six injuries involved the eye or eye area. There were three abrasions, one laceration, one hemorrhage and one hematoma. Four of the children did not require treatment beyond that provided in the emergency room. The other two were treated in the emergency room and were referred for further care.

We now had proof that Katie's accident was not an isolated event. Including our daughter's accident, there had been seven pegboard display-hook accidents to the eye or area surrounding the eye in the past 18 months.

If this type of accident could happen seven times in 18 months, it would surely happen again—it was just a matter of time before another, and possibly more serious, accident occurred.

According to the Centers for Disease Control in Atlanta, Georgia, 90% of injuries are predictable and preventable. The trick, though, is to get people to stop thinking of them as accidents or acts of fate.

By this time, I felt ready to go to the media. However, I decided that I would try to negotiate with the store one more time. Having received Mr. Smith's letter, I didn't think he was sympathetic with our concerns, and I wanted to negotiate with someone in the firm who had more power. I called Mr. "Roberts," President of "National" Department Stores. We called back and forth several times, but were unable to connect. By this time, the secretary at their head office knew who I was and suggested that I talk with Mr. Smith. I agreed to talk with him and asked that he call me in a half-hour. I felt that I needed that much time to prepare my arguments and to prepare myself emotionally because I felt so offended by his initial letter to us.

I also wanted to set my answering machine so I could record the conversation. I knew I could not use the conversation legally without informing Smith. However, this was an opportunity for me to debrief a negotiation that I felt incredibly strongly about. As I prepared, my wife counseled me to not let myself get angry and to not speak too quickly. The transcript of that conversation follows:

**Mr. Smith:** What would you like us to do?
**Brad McRae:** I would like to see all of those hooks removed from your stores.
**Smith:** I'm not sure that's practical—I'm not sure that that is practically possible.
**B.M.:** Are you willing to live with the risk that another child could get injured in one of your stores?
**Smith:** I'm not sure that is a fair question.
**B.M.:** Excuse me, sir, but how is that not a fair question?
**Smith:** I don't want to be a smart-ass, but frankly, we have more accidents on elevators and escalators than we do with pegboard display hooks.
**B.M.:** Excuse me, sir, but my daughter almost lost her eye in your store. In the past 18 months, according to the Children's Injury Program database, there have been over 19 display-related accidents to children in Canada. Six of these accidents were pegboard-hook-related acci-

dents to the eye or facial area near the eye. Two of the six cases required long-term treatment.

**Mr. Smith:** As parents, we are all responsible for our children. As Katie's father, you are partly responsible for her accident. [I almost lost my temper here but somehow managed to stay in the balcony and keep my perspective.]

**B.M.:** Excuse me, sir, if I had left Katie unattended at an elevator or escalator, I could see how I would be responsible, but one would assume that one was in a relatively safe environment in the main aisle of the store's shoe department.

Smith made no comment at this point, so I continued:

**B.M.:** I do not want to go to the press, but if you are not willing to make your stores safe for children, then I feel that you are forcing me to do so. If I didn't do everything possible to prevent future accidents of this type, I would feel that I was partially responsible.

**Smith:** Thank you for your time.

**B.M.:** Please have Mr. "Roberts" call me.

Mr. Roberts and I played telephone tag for two days. I was then told that he was out of the country. At this point, I gave up negotiating with National and called the local CBC television and radio stations, who agreed to do our story.

The local CBC television news crew came to our home and interviewed us, and our story was presented on the 6 pm evening news. Since we were one of the two lead stories, the lead anchor announced that they would be doing the story several times before it aired on television. The lead-off announcements and the story started with a photo taken right after Katie arrived home from the hospital. It showed her wearing an eye patch and drinking milk from a bottle. If a picture is worth a thousand words, this photo would make it very difficult for National's management not to address the issue of child safety.

The coverage was thorough and fair, and both sides were interviewed. On air, the manager of the local store said that all the display hooks in the store would be changed. On the morning before our story was televised, we received the following letter from Mr. Smith:

*December 18, 1991*

Dear Drs. McRae and Crosby,

On further reflection, we have decided to take action as quickly as possible to minimize risk to young children in our stores.

   1. Capping pegboard hooks

   2. Replacing hooks in department stores with "child appeal" with harm-proof equipment

   3. Removing the bottom rows of these hooks in some departments.

We believe such a program is our best effort to avoid a similar occurrence in the future.

Yours sincerely,

John Smith
Vice President of Operations

This was a typical 11th-hour settlement, and we were jubilant. One of Canada's major department stores stated publicly that it was going to change the way it displayed its merchandise and improve display safety in its stores. Would we have been able to get this type of response from the store without using the media? No. Going to the media was our BATNA (Best Alternative to a Negotiated Agreement). We felt that we had won our case, with CBC's help, from the jury of public opinion.

However, our victory was short-lived. I entered the store the following week, and only the display in the shoe section had been changed. All of the other pegboard display hooks remained unchanged. There were some 6,000 pegboard display hooks in this one store alone. Two months later, one-third of the hooks had plastic caps over their end points.

I wanted to be able to present a strong argument that the plastic caps were not a suitable solution for protecting people from injury. I contacted the head of pediatric ophthalmology from the local children's hospital, who said,

If a child running with a pencil in his or her hand trips, and the point of the pencil penetrates the eye, it will damage the eye. If the eraser hits the eye, it can also traumatize the eye. The advantage of the pencil over the pegboard hook is the pencil in the child's arm will move. The pegboard hook, which is attached to the wall, is potentially more lethal.

The pediatric ophthalmologist provided me with a more thorough justification for changing the hooks than I had. At the same time, we were using expert testimony, which would carry more weight.

By this time, I had also looked into the laws governing display safety in Canada and in the United States. Quite frankly, there were none. In Canada, there was legislation governing products through the Hazardous Products Act. There was no legislation governing displays. We have been working with Mary Clancy, our local member of Parliament; she sponsored a private members' bill to bring in legislation regarding display safety and is continuing to work on the initiative. However, the question becomes even more complicated when one considers the question of whether display safety is a national or a provincial responsibility. I will continue to work on getting legislation passed regarding display safety, and I will continue to inform the government of the number of display-related accidents that take place each year. It may take a great deal more time to bring this issue to fruition.

In the meantime, I contacted the provincial Department of Labor. If these displays could be a hazard to customers, they could also be a hazard to employees. The Department of Labor investigated Katie's accident and wrote a report. The report documented the fact that pegboard hooks had been the cause of several accidents to workers. The report also stated that there were three types of commercially available double-pronged hooks that were designed to be safer than the single-pronged hooks. The Department of Labor voiced its concern about the single-pronged hooks to the Canadian Retail Association and stated that that was the extent of the help they could give to our concerns.

We were getting nowhere fast. Our private members' bill had received its first reading in our national Parliament, and there was no telling if it would ever receive a second or third reading. (There are many private members' bills, and they are selected by lottery.)

I tried to get the local media to do a follow-up to the original story. I had hoped that the new publicity would help bring about some change. My wife and I had gone to the store with our camera to document the fact that the displays had not been changed. It was shocking to see that the single-pronged hooks, similar to the ones that had caused so many other accidents, were still in use throughout the store—except in the shoe department, where they had been replaced for the benefit of the television audience during the previous documentary report. We were upset to see the hooks still in use in the children's toy department and in the children's clothing section. Ironically, the hooks were used to display devices used in the home to increase children's safety and to prevent accidents.

The response from the local media was that "the story was a bit thin" and that "there would have to be another local accident before they would be interested in picking the story up again." I was incredulous. Accidents made good stories, but preventing them was apparently not significant enough to be newsworthy.

By now, eight months had passed since the accident, but we would not give up.

I thought the matter over and decided that we had two strategies:

- Strategy 1: Twenty mothers with young children in strollers were willing to picket the store with me. If we had to make a story to get media attention, we would.
- Strategy 2: We would try to get national coverage through CBC's *Marketplace* (a program similar to *Sixty Minutes* in the United States).

The second strategy worked. *Marketplace* agreed to tell our story. I was amazed when they spent over two hours interviewing and filming us for a 10-minute segment of the program. The program was masterfully done. They showed children playing and running in a store. They showed the hooks, so it was easy to see how accidents could occur. They also showed other stores and how they had installed the safer, dual-pronged display attachments.

I also decided to write to every member of the Board of Directors of the "National" Department Store about my concerns regarding child safety in their stores and asked them to watch the *Marketplace* documentary.

I went to the local library and looked up the annual report for "National" Department Store. This report listed the names of the members of the Board of Directors. A copy of that letter follows. Please note that in the letter I endeavored to increase the muscle level without becoming adversarial:

*November 10, 1992*


Dear Director of the "National" Department Store:


On November 9, 1991, my daughter, Kathryn McRae, sustained a serious eye injury when she approached a display of animal character slippers in the shoe department of your store. Unfortunately, the slippers were suspended by six-inch, single-pronged metal hooks. One of these hooks penetrated her eye. She is currently receiving ongoing medical treatment at the children's hospital.

Recently, there has been another display-related eye injury at the "National" Department Store. The child in question sustained no long-term trauma to the eye. However, it is just a matter of time until there is another injury with more serious consequences. In our efforts to bring public attention to this matter, CBC's *Marketplace* has agreed to do a story on display accidents in stores. The show is to air on November 24, 1992 at 7:30 p.m. My understanding is that the show will present the details of my daughter's accident, our attempt to bring this matter to the attention of the public, and your store's response to date.

Unfortunately, the type of hook that damaged my daughter's eye is still in wide use at your stores. I was told by Mr. Smith, Vice President of Operations, in his letters dated November 28 and December 18, 1991, that rubber caps would be placed over the hooks as an interim measure and that the bottom rows of these hooks would be removed in some departments.

I checked with Dr. LaRoche, the head of pediatric ophthalmology at the children's hospital, and he told me that the rubber caps which have been placed on some of the hooks in some of your stores are not an adequate solution, as they do nothing to prevent blunt eye injury. In fact, it was that force of the hook hitting the eye that has apparently caused either neurological or muscular damage to my daughter's eye. I also informed Mr. Smith and Mr. Roberts that my daughter's accident was not an isolated event. According to Health and Welfare's Bureau of Chronic Disease Epidemiology Laboratory Center for Disease Control, which has been keeping a database on all childhood injuries reported in children's hospital emergency rooms, there have been 19 display-related injuries in Canada, at least six of which were to the eye.

Three other major stores have changed all of their display hooks to double-pronged hooks. My understanding is that one of these stores changed all of the hooks five years ago.

I have great difficulty understanding the "National" Department Store's lack of response to this problem. There is no sign of the new hooks that I was told were on order a year ago. The "National" Department Store is risking the possibility that a potentially more serious eye injury could occur in one of your establishments. This issue has been raised once on CBC television locally, and three times on CBC radio, and now it will be raised on television nationally. If there were a serious display injury at one of your stores, after all of this media attention, the ensuing publicity would be very bad for the "National" Department Store, indeed.

It is also my understanding that, under director's liability, store officials could be held responsible, since the potential hazard is well known to officers of the "National" Department Store.

We do not wish to be adversarial, but so far our concerns have been not been addressed by the "National" Department Store in any significant manner. We want corrective action to be started now to replace the type of display hook that injured our daughter. Our commitment to the issue of childhood safety in retail stores is strong. If necessary, we will keep this issue before the public. We would, however, prefer to work cooperatively with the "National" Department Store to improve the safety of Canada's children.

Sincerely,

Brad McRae

It worked. On the morning that the *Marketplace* program went on the air, I received the following letter from the parent company of "National" Department Store:

*November 24, 1992*

Dear Drs. McRae & Crosby:

This will acknowledge receipt of your letter of November 12, 1992 regarding the accident suffered by your daughter in the "National" Department Store in Halifax. It has also come to my attention that you have forwarded a similar letter to members of the Board of Directors of the "National" Holding Company Ltd.

May I, on behalf of our Directors, express my sincere apology for the manner with which this issue has been addressed. There is no plausible excuse for not reacting quickly to the identified hazards in our stores, and I am sorry for the lack of good judgment used in this instance.

I have today been assured that the target date for crimping [bending back] all display hooks in the "National" Department Stores across Canada is December 1, 1992. We are also investigating whether this procedure is adequate to ensure safety; if not, an alternative fixture will be installed. Our "ABC" and "DEF" Stores have also been instructed to comply. As well, our Corporate Store Planning Department will insure that all new stores or renovations to existing stores will receive safe installations.

In the meantime, I thank you for bringing this matter to my attention; the public's safety in our stores is of paramount concern to the "National" Holding Company.

Yours sincerely,

President and Chief Executive Officer
"National" Holding Company

Several days later, I telephoned the president of "National" Holding Company and asked him if the company would be willing to provide other stores in Canada with a copy of the hand tool to help decrease the likelihood of further accidents of this type. He replied that the store would provide a copy of the hand tool at cost to member stores through the Retail Council of Canada. If I had been adversarial, it is much less likely that this would have occurred.

## Epilogue

At this point, I want to share with you what we have accomplished, what remains to be accomplished, and our strategy for proceeding from here.

In terms of accomplishment, first, "National" Department Store did change its display policy all across the country. Over 10 million single-pronged hooks have been bent back or changed to double-pronged butterfly hooks. Eventually, all the single-pronged hooks will be replaced by these safer double-pronged hooks. Second, the public's awareness of the danger of single-pronged display hooks has been raised through television and radio programs and through my public speaking and teaching on negotiation and influencing skills, as I frequently use this example to talk about coalitions, BATNAs, and muscle level. Third, the media and legal attention that our case has received makes it easier for other victims of this type of accident to ask for appropriate redress. Third, the Canadian Retail Council has made its members aware of the danger of single-pronged hooks and has published several articles on how to make displays safer. Fourth, safety organizations in each of the Canadian provinces have been notified about the dangers of single-pronged display hooks, and I have also written about my concerns to consumer advocate Ralph Nader in the United States.

In terms of what is left to accomplish, unsafe displays and indeed the whole issue of display safety are still not adequately addressed through legislation in either the United States or Canada. Every year, I collect information on additional display-hook injuries and display injuries in general. With this updated information, our member of Parliament is endeavoring to get a private members' bill passed to address the issue of display safety. Our strategy for the future is that the publication of this book will hopefully bring pressure on governments to work harder on the issue of display safety, for the Centers for Disease Control in the United States has determined that 90% of accidents are both predictable and preventable. We must do a better job of preventing needless accidents.

# Conclusion

▓ ▓ ▓ ▓

Learning effective negotiating and influencing skills is a life-long process. In a very real sense, reading this book is only the beginning of that process. To answer the question "Where do I go from here?" several suggestions are given in this chapter regarding books to read, courses to take, and the continuing use of the feedback forms provided in this book. Information is also presented on programs that teach negotiating and influencing skills in elementary schools and in high schools.

### Learning From Books

An annotated bibliography on negotiating and influencing skills is presented in Appendix A. Each book listed there is described in enough detail to help you make an informed choice about whether it can be of benefit to you in developing your skills further.

### Learning From Courses

Excellent courses are available through the Program on Negotiation at Harvard Law School, the MIT-Harvard Public Disputes Resolution Program, the Program on Instruction for Lawyers, and McRae Seminars. Each of these institutions and their course offerings are described below:

The *Program on Negotiation* at Harvard Law School offers a variety of excellent courses.

- One of the best is the "Program on Negotiation for Senior Executives." This one-and-a-half-day course is taught by three faculty members from the Program on Negotiation. The course helps the participants better understand the "Getting to Yes" model through both individual and team negotiation simulations. The simulations provide direct feedback on where your negotiation skills are working well and on where they need to be improved.
- Another highly recommended course is William Ury's "Dealing with Difficult People and Difficult Situations: New 'Mutual Gains' Strategies for Succeeding in Tough Negotiations." Ury is a master teacher. The course examines strategies and tactics that can be used against you in a negotiation and effective counterstrategies that you can use when negotiating with difficult people and in difficult situations.
- For those interested in teaching negotiation skills, the course "Teaching Negotiation in the Corporation" will be of interest. This course presents the developmental history and the pedagogy of teaching negotiation skills as taught in Harvard's Program on Negotiation.
- For those interested in complex multiple-party, value-laden disputes, I highly recommend "Dealing With an Angry Public: Protecting Your Reputation and Your Market Share." This course deals with strategies for "resolving conflicts and disputes with dissatisfied customers, potential litigants, and concerned interest groups."

For more detailed information on these and other course offerings, contact:

Program on Negotiation
Harvard Law School
Cambridge, MA 02138

Phone (617) 495-1111, Fax (617) 495-1546
email: http://www.law.harvard.edu.programs.pon

The *Program of Instruction for Lawyers* offers two intensive five-day courses every June: the Basic Course and the Advanced Course. Approximately 60% of the student enrollment is from the United States, with the remaining 40% from other countries. Two-thirds to three-quarters of the students are lawyers; the rest are from various other backgrounds. Being a lawyer is not a prerequisite. The course members spend a great deal of time negotiating. Many of the case studies are scorable, so the participants receive immediate feedback as to how well they negotiated compared to others. A highlight of each course is the use of Harvard's advanced technique of videotaped feedback. The length of the course and the sheer number of negotiations that take place ensure that participants see where they are negotiating well and where improvement is required.

For more information on this program, contact:

Program of Instruction for Lawyers
Harvard Law School
207 Pound Hall
Cambridge, MA 02138

Phone (617) 495-3187

*McRae Seminars* offers basic and advanced courses on "Effective Negotiating and Influencing Skills," "Mediation Skills in Business and Organizational Settings," and the "Consensus Decision-Making Workshop." Custom-designed courses are also available to meet an organization's specific needs and requirements.

For more information on these seminars, contact:

McRae Seminars
5880 Spring Garden Road, Suite 400
Halifax, Nova Scotia B3H 1Y1 Canada

Phone (902) 423-4680
email: bmcrae@ns.sympatico.ca
website: http://www 3.ns.sympatico.ca\bmcrae

### Learning From Exercises and Inventories

Doing and redoing the exercises and inventories in this book will also prove helpful. A copy of each of the exercises and inventories cited in this book appears in Appendix B.

**Learning From Mentors and Peers**

Finding and using a negotiation mentor(s) will help you develop your negotiating and influencing skills. Forming a peer support group is also an excellent idea. The peer support group that I belong to meets one evening per month. The members of the group also talk with each other during the month to provide ongoing support and coaching.

**Negotiation/Mediation Programs in Schools**

An increasing number of schools are teaching negotiating and influencing skills as part of their curriculum. In these schools, children are explicitly taught, from kindergarten age on, to understand others' feelings and reach consensus in resolving conflicts. Five-year-olds' fights are stopped and the children are asked, "What is (the other child) feeling right now? What does he or she want? What are you feeling? What do you want? What can you suggest that will help you to get both of your needs met?"

For example, in an "Orange Shirt" program, children are taught negotiating, influencing and peace-making skills. Every day, a different child wears the orange shirt. If there is a dispute on the playground, the child in the orange shirt asks the disputants if they want him or her to intervene. If the answer is no, the disputants continue to resolve the dispute on their own, and/or a teacher might intervene. If the disputants say yes, the child in the orange shirt negotiates agreement to these four rules:

- You have to listen.
- You have to tell the truth.
- You can't fight.
- You can't run away.

Studies have shown that there is an increase in attendance and a decrease in violence in schools where peace-making initiatives have been introduced. One study showed that, among delinquent boys who became mediators, there was an increase in the percentage of delinquent boys who graduated from high school and the percentage who went on to attend college.

Here is an example of the effect that peer mediation programs can have in schools:

In the 1960s, there was a great debate about the virtues of closing small high schools and building larger regional high schools. The advantages of the bigger school were due to economies of scale. Where several small schools could not afford to have a modern science lab, the larger school could. However, research reported in Berker's (1964) book *Big School/Small School* found that there were also some disadvantages associated in moving to a larger school. One of the major disadvantages was the loss in the number of roles that the students could play.

In the smaller schools, there were more opportunities for a student to be president of the student body, captain of the football team, member of the debating society, and member of the school service club, among others, because there were fewer numbers of students for each potential role. There is also clear evidence that students' growth is related not only to what they learn in school but also to the roles they play and the learnings derived from being in those roles.

The role of mediator in school-sponsored peer mediation programs is an important addition to the traditional roles available to students. The following example attests to the powerful learning that can take place in the mediator's role.

Jim has two children: Paul in Grade 9, and Kate in Grade 6. Jim describes his son as a very gregarious child and an excellent student and athlete. All three of these roles supported Paul's good sense of self-esteem at school. Jim describes his daughter as a good student, friendly, caring and compassionate, and having "two left feet" when it comes to athletics. The nature of the school and of the children in it seemed to accord more value to Paul's characteristics than to Kate's. In fact, Jim was concerned that living in the shadow of her older brother was having a negative effect on Kate's self-esteem.

The school started a peer mediation program last fall. Kate applied and was accepted. The training and experience of being a peer mediator support her unique talents. At the dinner table, Kate readily talks about her cases—what went well and what was difficult—with the same sense of purpose and pride as Paul talks about his successes and failures on the soccer and baseball fields and at the hockey rink.

Jim tells me that he has had some very interesting discussions with Kate about negotiating and mediating, developing alternative solutions, and strategizing ways to help shape agreements. Jim says that this experience, more than anything else in the past four years, has helped give Kate a positive sense of herself and of the skills and talents that she has developed.

Negotiating and mediating skills are among the most important skills you can learn. Peer mediation programs in schools provide the roles, the training, and the experience to help children learn these important skills.

**If You Want to Learn More About Negotiating and Influencing Skills**

There are excellent videos, reference books, and case simulations available from the Program on Negotiation Clearinghouse. Most of the videos are available for screening at a very reasonable cost, and the books and case studies are usually delivered to you within a week's time. For a list of their offerings and prices, contact:

Program on Negotiation Clearinghouse
Harvard Law School
518 Pound Hall
Cambridge, MA 02138

Phone (617) 495-1684, Fax (617) 495-7818
email: http://www.law.harvard.edu.programs.pon

Many excellent resources on negotiation, mediation, and conflict management are also available through the Network on Conflict Resolution. For information, contact:

Network on Conflict Resolution
Conrad Grebel College
Waterloo, Ontario N2L 3G6 Canada

Phone (519) 885-0880, Fax (519) 885-0860
email: nicr@watserv1.uwaterloo.ca
        http://watserv1.uwaterloo.ca:80/ ~nier

In closing, I wish you every success in developing your own negotiating and influencing skills in your professional and personal life. It is also my hope that, both by example and through coaching and mentoring, you will teach others the art of creating and claiming value so that the world can truly be a better place.

# Appendix A

## Annotated Bibliography

❊ Axelrod, R. (1984). *The evolution of cooperation.* New York: Basic Books.

This is an academic book about the conditions under which cooperation evolves. It offers valuable insights illustrated by wonderful examples. Among the best is the description about how the English and German armies cooperated to minimize the chance of death and injury to both sides during the trench warfare of World War I—that is, until the generals on both sides put a stop to it. You may find this book somewhat difficult to read in parts; so consider reading only the parts that you find worthwhile.

❊ Carter, J. (1989). *Nasty people: How to stop being hurt by them without becoming one of them.* New York: Contemporary Books.

This is an excellent little book on dealing with difficult people, particularly on how to disarm them.

❊ Fisher, R., & Brown, S. (1988). *Getting together: Building a relationship that gets to yes.* Boston: Houghton Mifflin.

This book adds excellent insights on the importance of relationship building to the "Getting to Yes" model. It is available through the Harvard Program on Negotiation Clearinghouse and the Network on Conflict Resolution.

❊ Fisher, R., & Ury, W. (1981). *Getting to yes: Negotiating agreement without giving in.* New York: Penguin Books.

*Getting to Yes* is the most widely read book on the subject of negotiation. It explains the philosophy behind principle-based/interest-based negotiating. *Getting to Yes* is a must-read for anyone interested in improving his or her understanding of the negotiating process. The second edition also contains a section on the 10 most frequently asked questions about the "Getting To Yes" approach. This book is available at most bookstores. It can also be ordered through the Harvard Program on Negotiation and the Network on Conflict Resolution.

- Hall, L. (Ed.). (1993). *Negotiation: Strategies for mutual gain.* Newbury Park: Sage.

*Negotiation* is a collection of articles by people who have taught at the Harvard Program on Negotiation. The book covers a wide variety of topics from labor management negotiations to resolving environmental disputes. The book is well written and is a good introduction to the 12 authors who have contributed their work. (Available through the Harvard Program on Negotiation)

- Kolb, D., & Associates. (1994). *When talk works: Profiles of mediators.* San Francisco: Jossey-Bass.

This book consists of a series of in-depth interviews with 12 of the world's best mediation practitioners. The fields in which these mediators work is quite broad. Among the areas covered are mediating business disputes, family and divorce mediation, labor grievances, international mediation, and peacemaking in a civil war.

Each practitioner is asked to describe the type of work they do and how each person developed his or her particular approach to and style of mediation, all of which leads to some very fascinating behind-the-scenes examples. One of the most interesting is reading about how President Carter used his skills in preparation and persuasion in negotiating the Camp David Accord between Israel and Egypt. This book is a must-read for anyone interested in developing insight into the mediation process. (Available through the Harvard Program on Negotiation Clearinghouse)

- Lax, D. A., & Sebenius, J. K. (1986). *The manager as negotiator: Bargaining for cooperation and competitive gain.* New York: Free Press.

This book is devoted to negotiating in business and organizational settings. It is also where I first read about the core concepts of creating and claiming value. The book is well written and contains a wealth of information. You should note that this is a very academic read and may take some time to get through. However, it is worth the effort. (Available through the Harvard Program on Negotiation Clearinghouse)

■ Pruitt, D., & Rubin, J. (1986). *Social conflict: Escalation, stalemate, and settlement.* New York: Random House.

This book is a classic on conflict resolution. It looks at conflict as if it were a three-act play. Act 1 is escalation, Act 2 is stalemate, and Act 3 is resolution to the conflict. This book contains a lot of information on the theory of conflict and conflict resolution, and, wherever possible, the theory is supported by applied research. This book is also very well written, although it may be too academic for some. (Available through the Harvard Program on Negotiation)

■ Rackham, N. (1984). *The psychology of negotiating* (Listen & Learn Tape No. T35). (Available from Listen & Learn Cassettes, Box 344 Station M, Toronto, Ontario, M6S 4T6, Canada)

Some audiotapes are worth listening to and others aren't. This one certainly is. It is particularly insightful about the characteristics of effective negotiators and their less effective counterparts.

■ Susskind, L., & Cruikshank, J. (1988). *Breaking the impasse: Consensual approaches to resolving public disputes.* New York: Basic Books.

*Breaking the Impasse* is a classic in the field of dispute resolution. It describes a three-part model designed to help multiple parties resolve value-laden disputes where the participants to the dispute often have entrenched positions. Well-described case studies illustrate the concepts. This book is a must-read for anyone interested in mediating disputes. (Available through the Harvard Program on Negotiation and the Network on Conflict Resolution)

■ Susskind, L., & Field, P. (1996). *Dealing with the angry public: The mutual gains approach to resolving disputes.* New York: Free Press.

This book develops and documents the use of the mutual gains approach for resolving multiple-party, value-based disputes. It contains detailed examples illustrating how this approach has helped resolve entrenched disputes more successfully than the more traditional approach of keeping information and power out of the hands of the public, which tends to exacerbate the problem.

For example, the authors demonstrate how the Exxon *Valdez* oil spill not only cost millions of dollars more than it should have but divided the Prince William Sound community into those who were overcompensated (some fishermen and clean-up contractors) and those who were undercompensated (Native Americans and recreational fishing store owners). A second example documents the Dow Corning breast implant controversy and how the ensuring lawsuits eventually forced the company into bankruptcy. The third example is the fascinating account of how the Quebec government of Bourassa and Hydro Quebec mishandled the James Bay II development by not taking the interests of the First Nations people into account. To their credit, Susskind and Field go beyond criticizing these organizations for mishandling the situations; they suggest how these situations could have been better handled by using the mutual gains approach.

My opinion as a practitioner and as a teacher in the field of conflict resolution is that this book is a must-read. It is articulately written and presents detailed case studies to help you understand the principles of consensus decision making between groups whose interests appear to be extremely adversarial. The book presents clear guidelines of what to do and what not to do to de-escalate differences and foster the consensus decision-making process. (Available through the Harvard Program on Negotiation and and the Network on Conflict Resolution)

▦   Ury, W. (1991). *Getting past no: Dealing with difficult people.* New York: Bantam Books.

I have seen William Ury negotiate, and he is indeed a master negotiator. How does he do it? Ury looks at problems as if they were multifaceted diamonds. He is able to look at problems from every viewplane of that diamond without becoming emotionally hooked into any of them. He is also able to move from viewplane to viewplane with the same fluidity with which a champion hockey player skates. Ury's abilities as a negotiator and a problem solver and the five-part method he employs are fully explained in this wonderful book. Ury himself describes this book as follows: "If *Getting to Yes* is how to do the negotiation dance, then *Getting Past No* explains how to get that reluctant dance partner onto the dance floor."

This book is a must-read if you want to better understand the negotiating process and learn about strategies and techniques to improve your skills. (Available through the Harvard Program on Negotiation and the Network on Conflict Resolution)

■   Ury, W. L., Brett, J. M., & Goldberg, S. B. (1993). *Getting disputes resolved: Designing systems to cut the costs of conflict.* Cambridge, MA: Harvard Program on Negotiation.

As the title indicates, this book is about designing systems to help resolve disputes. One of the principles of Total Quality Management is that 85% of work-site problems are procedural and only 15% are due to the people involved. Therefore, if we can develop better procedures, we can systematically lessen the number of disputes and put into place better mechanisms for resolving them. This book has excellent examples that help illustrate the principles involved. (Available through the Harvard Program on Negotiation and the Network on Conflict Resolution)

# Appendix B

## Exercises and Forms

▦ ▦ ▦ ▦

Duplicates of exercises and forms presented throughout the book are combined here to use in monitoring your progress toward bettering your negotiating skills.

▦ ▦ ▦ ▦

### EXERCISE 1.1
### Negotiation Survey

1. Estimate the percentage of time you spend negotiating on your job, with "negotiating" being defined quite broadly. The definition I prefer is that a negotiation is any communication between people in which one or both parties has a goal in mind. For instance, if you were communicating with an employee about arriving at the job on time, that communication is defined as a negotiation. With this definition in mind, estimate the percentage of time, from 0% to 99%, that you spend negotiating at work: _____.

2. Rate your effectiveness as a negotiator at work on a scale from 1 to 10, where 1 is "very ineffective" and 10 is "very effective." For example, rating yourself a 1 could indicate that you give in on all of your interests to keep the peace or, alternatively, that you never back down and that most of your negotiations escalate into a fight. Rating yourself a 10 means that you possess the wisdom of Solomon and can successfully negotiate a flawless settlement for every conflict: _____.

3. What will be the biggest challenge facing you in your business/professional career in the coming year?

4. Rate your effectiveness as a negotiator in your personal life outside work on a scale from 1 to 10, where 1 is "very ineffective" and 10 is "very effective." Again, rating yourself a 1 could indicate that you give in on all of your interests to keep the peace or, alternatively, that you never back down and that most of your negotiations escalate into a fight. Rating yourself a 10 means that you possess the wisdom of Solomon and can successfully negotiate a perfect settlement for every conflict: _____.

5. What will be the biggest challenge facing you in your personal life in the coming year?

6. What would you like to learn or how would you like to be able to negotiate differently as a result of reading this book and improving your own negotiating skills?

7. What advantages would accrue to you from becoming a better negotiator?

8. What advantages would accrue to your company or organization from your becoming a better negotiator?

■  ■  ■  ■

## EXERCISE 2.1
### Creating and Claiming Value

1.  Think of the last negotiation you were in. Summarize that negotiation in the space provided below:




2.  Rate yourself from 1 to 10 on how well you created value in that negotiation, where 1 is "created little or no value" and 10 is "created a great deal of value."

   My effectiveness in creating value in my last negotiation was: _____

3.  Next, rate yourself from 1 to 10 on how well you claimed value in your last negotiation, where 1 represents "obtained little or no value for myself" and 10 represents "obtained a great deal of value for myself."

   My effectiveness in claiming value in my last negotiation was: _____

The next step is to study how you create and claim value in your next three negotiations. This will help you determine your own pattern in creating and claiming value. To be an effective negotiator, you have to be good at both creating and claiming value. The following form has been designed to help you examine your own pattern of creating and claiming value.

### CREATING/CLAIMING VALUE FORM

1.  Briefly summarize a negotiation that you participated in.
   Rate your effectiveness in creating value (1-10):     _____
   Rate your effectiveness in claiming value (1-10):     _____

2.  Briefly summarize another negotiation.
   Rate your effectiveness in creating value (1-10):     _____
   Rate your effectiveness in claiming value (1-10):     _____

3. Briefly summarize another negotiation.

   Rate your effectiveness in creating value (1-10):    _____

   Rate your effectiveness in claiming value (1-10):    _____

4. From your observations in these three negotiations, what do you do well in the area of creating value?

5. From your observations in these three negotiations, what specifically do you need to do to improve your skills in creating value?

6. From your observations in these three negotiations, what do you do well in the area of claiming value?

7. From your observations in these three negotiations, what specifically do you need to do to improve your skills in claiming value?

■ ■ ■ ■

**EXERCISE 3.1**
**Rating Your Competencies**

You now have the opportunity to rate yourself on these eight critical competencies. The following competencies survey will help alert you to the areas in which your negotiating skills most need to be developed. To perform this test, rate yourself with an "X" on the following 10-point scales, in which 1 is indicative of a low level of skill development and 10 is indicative of a high level of skill development:

## Rating Your Intellectual Competencies

1. *Planning/Causal Thinking:* "Planning/causal thinking is hypothesis gen-eration, essentially. It involves seeing either the potential implication of events or the likely consequences of a situation based on what has usually happened in the past." (Klemp & McClelland, cited in Sternberg & Wagner, 1986, p. 40)

| I do not enjoy nor am I good at developing hypotheses and seeing the consequences for a situation based on what has happened in the past. | I enjoy and I am good at developing hypotheses and seeing the consequences for a situation based on past events. |
|---|---|

|   |   |   |   |   |   |   |   |   |   |
|---|---|---|---|---|---|---|---|---|---|
| 1 | 2 | 3 | 4 | 5 | 6 | 7 | 8 | 9 | 10 |

2. *Diagnostic Information Seeking:* Diagnostic information-seeking is push-ing for concrete data in all sorts of ways, using a variety of sources to get as much information as possible to help with solving a particular prob- lem. People who are good at diagnostic information-seeking are naturally curious and they ask questions to help them get the most data/information possible.

| I do not typically ask very many questions nor am I seen by others to engage in a great deal of diagnostic information seeking. | I typically ask a great many questions. Others see me engage in a great deal of diagnostic information seeking. |
|---|---|

|   |   |   |   |   |   |   |   |   |   |
|---|---|---|---|---|---|---|---|---|---|
| 1 | 2 | 3 | 4 | 5 | 6 | 7 | 8 | 9 | 10 |

3. *Conceptualization/Synthetic Thinking:* "Conceptualization/synthetic think-ing is theory-building in order to account for consistent patterns in recurring events or for connections between seemingly unrelated pieces of informa-tion; it is enhanced by diagnostic information-seeking." (p. 40)

I am not good at nor do I enjoy building theories from seemingly unrelated events or data.

I am good at and I enjoy building theories from seemingly unrelated or data.

1 2 3 4 5 6 7 8 9 10

## Rating Your Influence Competencies

4. *Need or Desire to Influence Others:* The need for influence is "an alertness to the potentialities for influencing others. Concern for influence appears in such statements as 'When I walked into that meeting, I was trying to figure out how to persuade them to agree to my proposal.' " (p. 40)

I do not have a strong need or desire to influence others.

I have a strong need or desire to influence others.

1 2 3 4 5 6 7 8 9 10

5. *Directive Influence:* Directive influence measures the ability to "confront people directly when problems occur, [to tell] people to do things the way [you want] them done." (p. 41)

I am not comfortable using my personal authority or expert power to make sure that something gets done.

I am comfortable using my personal authority or expert power to make sure that something gets done.

1 2 3 4 5 6 7 8 9 10

6. *Collaborative Influence:* Collaborative influence measures the ability to operate "effectively with groups to influence outcomes and get cooperation, [to build] 'ownership' . . . among key subordinates by involving them in decision making." (p. 41)

| I need improvement at building relationships for the good of both parties. | I am good at building relationships for the good of both parties. |

| 1 | 2 | 3 | 4 | 5 | 6 | 7 | 8 | 9 | 10 |

7. *Symbolic Influence:* This last influence competency "is indicated by a use of symbols to influence how people act in the organization. A senior manager with this competency can, by personal example or a statement of mission, create a sense of purpose for the whole organization, which engenders individuals' loyalty and commitment to it." (p. 42)

| I have difficulty leading others by enrolling them with a sense of mission. | I can easily lead others by enrolling them with a sense of mission. |

| 1 | 2 | 3 | 4 | 5 | 6 | 7 | 8 | 9 | 10 |

### Rating Your Self-Confidence Competency

8. *Self-Confidence:* Managers with strength in this competency, "although recognizing difficulties, never express any doubt that they will ultimately succeed. In behavioral interviews, they display strong self-presentation skills and come across as very much in charge. They act to make others feel comfortable, and they respond quickly and confidently to requests in key situations. By contrast, average senior managers are more tentative. Moreover, outstanding managers express self-confidence by being stimulated by crises and other problems rather than distressed or overwhelmed by them." (p. 42)

| I have a low degree of self-confidence. | I have a high degree of self-confidence. |

| 1 | 2 | 3 | 4 | 5 | 6 | 7 | 8 | 9 | 10 |

■  ■  ■  ■

## EXERCISE 3.2
### Skill Development Plan

The three skills that I will develop further are:

1. _____

   Development Plan:

2. _____

   Development Plan:

3. _____

   Development Plan:

■  ■  ■  ■

## EXERCISE 3.3
### Negotiation Feedback Form

List three things that you like about _____'s
negotiating style. Please be as specific as possible. Simply saying "John
is a good communicator" is not specific enough. It should be so specific
that John will know exactly what he should do more of in the future.
For example, a specific comment would be "John is very good at coming
up with creative solutions. He always invents at least three options to
be considered at every negotiation."

1.


2.


3. Please list three specific targets for improving _____'s
negotiating style:

    a.

    b.

    c.


■ ■ ■ ■

**EXERCISE 3.4**
**Integrated Assessment**


1. What are three areas these instruments agree on in relation to your
negotiation strengths?

    a.

    b.

    c.


2. What are three areas these instruments agree on for improvement in
your negotiation style?

    a.

    b.

    c.


3. Were there any questions raised about your negotiation style that need
further clarification, understanding, and/or more information/data before
you can improve them?

███ ███ ███ ███

## EXERCISE 4.1
### Improving Fact Finding

1. In the space below, briefly describe a situation in which not having all the facts caused you to be a less effective negotiator than you could have been.

2. What do you have to do to better gather all the necessary facts in the future?

███ ███ ███ ███

## EXERCISE 4.2
### Developing Opening Statements

Using the preceding as a model, write an effective opening statement for a negotiation you are in now or are about to enter. Critique your opening statement on mutual benefits, core values or principles, use of superordinate goal(s), benefits to negotiating, and/or the cost of not negotiating. Then ask several good negotiators to critique your opening statements from time to time.

■  ■  ■  ■

## EXERCISE 4.3
### Asking High-Yield Questions

Observe several of the best negotiators you know. Watch how they use high-yield questions. What have you learned that will increase your effectiveness in asking high-yield questions? In the space below, write down what you have learned and then prepare several high-yield questions for your next negotiation.

■  ■  ■  ■

## EXERCISE 4.4
### Effective Pausing

Observe the people you are negotiating with. Who pauses effectively? Who does not? What effect does pausing and not pausing have? Next, observe yourself negotiating. When do you pause effectively? When don't you?

■  ■  ■  ■

## EXERCISE 4.5
### Turning Issues Into Interests

For the purpose of this exercise, please use the worksheet below to identify all the interests for all parties in a negotiation you are currently in or use it to help you prepare for an upcoming negotiation.

## TURNING ISSUES INTO INTERESTS

Issues for Party #1                              Issues for Party #2


Interests for Party #1                           Interests for Party #2

  1.                                               1.

  2.                                               2.

  3.                                               3.

  4.                                               4.

  5.                                               5.

  6.                                               6.

  7.                                               7.

  8.                                               8.

  9.                                               9.

 10.                                              10.


■  ■  ■  ■

### EXERCISE 4.6
### Identifying Additional and Hidden Interests

Think of three negotiations where you, or the party you were negotiating with, or another person looked for and discovered additional interests that made it possible to reach an agreement.

1.

2.

3.

What have you learned from this exercise that will make it more likely that you will discover and add additional interests in your future negotiations?

◼ ◼ ◼ ◼

## EXERCISE 4.7
### Using the Appropriate Muscle Level

1. Note a recent situation in which you escalated your muscle level too soon.

2. What were the negative consequences of escalating too quickly?

3. What would you do differently next time?

◼ ◼ ◼ ◼

## EXERCISE 4.8
### Using the Appropriate Muscle Level

1. Note a recent situation in which you did not escalate your use of power quickly enough.

2. What were the negative consequences of not using enough power soon enough?

3. What would you do differently next time?

■ ■ ■ ■

**EXERCISE 4.9**
**Taking Appropriate Breaks From the Table**

1. In the space below, outline a negotiation in which you did not do as well as you could have.

2. Next, describe how a break from the table and/or reopening the nego-tiation could have helped you to negotiate more effectively.

■ ■ ■ ■

**EXERCISE 4.10**
**Using the Power of Balance**

Give an example of a negotiation in which you used the power of balance to equalize the power of the parties.

▓ ▓ ▓ ▓

**EXERCISE 4.11**
**Using the Power of Balance**

1. Describe a negotiation in which you should have used the power of balance but did not.

2. What would you do differently if you had the chance to renegotiate the above situation?

▓ ▓ ▓ ▓

**EXERCISE 4.12**
**Using the Power of the Apology to**
**Get the Negotiation Back on Track**

1. Think of three times when you apologized during the course of a negotiation with the end result being that you furthered the negotiation process.

    a.

    b.

    c.

2. List specific characteristics of situations where apologizing works for you.

3. How could you use an apology more often to resolve problems and build relationships in your future negotiations?

4. Think of three times when you apologized during the course of a negotiation and it worked against you.

   a.

   b.

   c.

5. List specific characteristics of situations where apologizing worked against you.

6. Based on the above, when should you apologize less often in your future negotiations?

### EXERCISE 5.1
### The Power of Perspective Management

In the space below, describe three situations in which you successfully used perspective management and kept your perspective when negotiating with a difficult person or in negotiating a difficult situation:

1.

2.

3.

░ ░ ░ ░

**EXERCISE 5.2**
**The Cost of Not Using Perspective Management**

In the space below, describe three situations in which you were not successful in using perspective management and you lost your perspective when negotiating with a difficult person or in a difficult situation:

1.

2.

3.

░ ░ ░ ░

**EXERCISE 5.3**
**Using Perspective Management More Effectively**

In reviewing these six situations, what have you learned about perspective management that will help you to keep your perspective and negotiate more effectively in the future?

* * * *

**EXERCISE 5.4**
**Identification of Core Values**

1. In the space provided, briefly describe a situation that was difficult for you.

Was there a core value(s) that had me hooked in this particular negotiation? If so, name the core value(s):

_____     _____

_____

If you need help in identifying the core value(s), who would be a good person(s) to contact?

_____     _____

Last, how do you need to modify the way you use this core value to ensure that it continues to work for you in those situations where it should and keep you from using it in situations where it has worked against you?

2. Briefly describe a situation that was difficult for you.

Was there a core value(s) that had you hooked in this particular negotiation? If so, name the core value(s):

_____     _____

_____

If you need help in identifying the core value(s), who would be a good person(s) to contact?

_____    _____

Last, how do you need to modify the way you use this core value to ensure that it will continue to work for you in those situations where it should and keep you from using it in situations where it has worked against you?

3. Briefly describe a situation that was difficult for you.

Was there a core value(s) that had you hooked in this particular negotiation? If so, name the core value(s):

_____    _____

_____

If you need help in identifying the core value(s), who would be a good person(s) to contact?

_____    _____

Last, do you need to modify the way you use one or more of the core value(s) identified in this exercise to ensure that they will work for you in those situations where they should and keep you from using them in situations where they have worked against you?

■  ■  ■  ■

## EXERCISE 5.5
### Modifying Core Values

1. List the core values you have identified that need to be modified.

2. How do they need to be modified so you can negotiate more effectively?

■  ■  ■  ■

## EXERCISE 5.6
### Identification of Core Beliefs

■ I must be loved or accepted by everyone.
■ I must be perfect in all I do.
■ All the people with whom I work or live must be perfect.
■ I can have little control over what happens to me.
■ It is easier to avoid facing difficulties and responsibilities than to deal with them.
■ Disagreement and conflict should be avoided at all costs.
■ People, including me, do not change.
■ Some people are always good; others are always bad.
■ The world should be perfect, and it is terrible and catastropher when it is not.
■ People are fragile and need to be protected from "the Truth."
■ Other people exist to make me happy, and cannot be happy unless others make me happy.

- Crises are invariably destructive, and no good can come from them.
- Somewhere there is the perfect job, the perfect "solution," the perfect partner, and so on, and all I need to do is search for them.
- I should not have problems. If I do, it indicates I am incompetent.
- There is one and only one way of seeing any situation—the "true" way.

Remember the last time you felt bad about something? What were you telling yourself? Were any of these 15 beliefs the basis for your self-talk?

Now, you are going to challenge the destructive self-talk that caused you those difficulties. For the event you have just thought about, write down your self-destructive talk in your own' words. It may well include self-condemnation and be full of what people should or ought to do. (Appendix B contains an additional copy for future use.)

## MY SELF-DEFEATING BELIEF

The event:

What I felt:

What I was telling myself:

What I did:

What my self-defeating belief(s) was (were):

---

*Author's Note:* This exercise was adapted from Ellis and Harper (1975).

Now, you are going to challenge your negative self-talk. You can challenge that negative core belief by re-interpreting it and by exchanging the shoulds and oughts for preferences for how you would like things to be. Or you can ask yourself what you can learn from that experience and how you could behave differently next time by filling in the table below.

My constructive self-talk would be:

My feelings would be:

My actions could be:

■ ■ ■ ■

## EXERCISE 5.7
### Anger Management Form

1. How intense am I going to allow my anger to become?

2. How long am I going to stay angry?

3. How am I going to use my anger constructively?

▓  ▓  ▓  ▓

## EXERCISE 5.8
### Self-Control Form

1. Describe a negotiation in which you demonstrated excellent self-control.

What role were you playing in the above situation that helped you maintain good self-control?

2. Describe another negotiation in which you demonstrated excellent self-control.

What role were you playing in the above situation that helped you maintain good self-control?

3. Describe yet another negotiation in which you demonstrated excellent self-control.

What role were you playing in the above situation that helped you maintain good self-control?

## EXERCISE 5.9
### Identification of Positive Roles

At this point, you have identified several situations in which you demonstrated excellent self-control in selected negotiations. You have also identified the "roles" you were playing in these negotiations that helped you maintain good self-control. In the space below, make a list of the positive "roles" that you can use on a more conscious and consistent basis to help you negotiate more effectively in the future:

## EXERCISE 5.10
### Improving Self-Control Form

1. Describe a negotiation in which you demonstrated poor self-control.

What role were you playing in the above situation that prevented you from maintaining good self-control?

2. Describe another negotiation in which you demonstrated poor self-control.

What role were you playing in the above situation that prevented you from maintaining good self-control?

3. Describe yet another negotiation in which you demonstrated poor self-control.

What role were you playing in the above situation that prevented you from maintaining good self-control?

■   ■   ■   ■

## EXERCISE 5.11
### Identifying Negative Roles

At this point, you have identified several situations in which you were not able to demonstrate good self-control in selected negotiations. You have also identified the "roles" you were playing in these negotiations that prevented you from maintaining good self-control. In the space below, please list the negative "roles" that you played:

To negotiate more effectively in the future, you need to make a conscious effort not to fall into these roles.

▓  ▓  ▓  ▓

## EXERCISE 5.12
### Case Study Analysis

Name three things that Bill did well in this negotiation.

1.


2.


3.


Based on what you know about the above situation, is there anything you would do differently?


▓  ▓  ▓  ▓

## EXERCISE 5.13
### The Power of Looking for Reasonable People

In the space below, describe a situation in which you used the power of looking for reasonable people to bring about a positive outcome to a difficult situation:

▨  ▨  ▨  ▨

**EXERCISE 5.14**
**The Power of Doing the Unexpected**

1. In the space below, describe a situation in which you used the power of the unexpected to help move a negotiation forward toward resolution.

▨  ▨  ▨  ▨

**EXERCISE 5.15**
**Shortening Recovery Time**

1. Give an example of how talking to someone who acted in the role of a recovery coach helped shorten your recovery time:

2. Effective negotiators have at least four people with whom they can talk who are very effective in helping them learn from their mistakes and reduce their recovery time. In the space below, list four people you can turn to who can help you learn from your mistakes and reduce your recovery time:

■ ■ ■ ■

## EXERCISE 6.1
### Identifying Frames

Describe a situation in which you used another person's "frame" successfully to help further your own interests.

■ ■ ■ ■

## EXERCISE 6.2
### Using Frames to Persuade

Can you think of a current situation in which you need to do a better job of using the power of active listening? By using the other party's frame, how might you reframe that particular situation to increase the likelihood that the other party will be able to see a solution to your mutual interests within his or her reframed perspective?

■ ■ ■ ■

## EXERCISE 6.3
### Writing a Sample Dialogue

**What I Felt or Thought**                    **What the Participants Said**

## EXERCISE 6.4
### Integrating Skills

In the space below, pick two skills that you would like to work on simultaneously—for example, active listening and assertiveness, creating value and claiming value, or being persuasive and being open to persuasion. Then develop a plan using the P.R.I.C.E. method or any other method to help ensure that you accomplish this very important and very difficult task.

## EXERCISE 6.5
### My New Approach

Write a brief memo (three to four paragraphs) to yourself, outlining your new approach to negotiating.

# References

■ ■ ■ ■

Axelrod, R. (1984). *The evolution of cooperation.* New York: Basic Books.

Bacow, L. S., & Wheeler, M. (1984). *Environmental dispute resolution.* New York: Plenum.

Bell, R. (1984). *You can win at office politics.* New York: Times Books.

Berker, R. G. (1964). *Big school, small school: High school size and student behavior.* Stanford, CA: Stanford University Press.

Bernstein, L. (1959). *The joy of music.* New York: Simon & Schuster.

Blanchard, K. H., & Lorber, R. L. (1984). *Putting the one minute manager to work.* New York: William Morrow.

Breslin, W., & Rubin, J. (Eds.). (1991). *Negotiation theory and practice.* Cambridge, MA: Harvard Program on Negotiation.

Burns, D. (1989). *The feeling good handbook.* New York: Penguin.

Carter, J. (1989). *Nasty people: How to stop being hurt by them without becoming one of them.* New York: Contemporary Books.

Cava, R. (1990). *Difficult people: How to deal with impossible clients, bosses and employees.* Toronto: Key Porter Books.

Cialdini, R. (1984). *Influence: How and why people agree to things.* New York: William Morrow.

Cohen, H. (1980). *You can negotiate anything.* Secaucua, NJ: Lyle Stuart.

Cornelius, H., & Faire, S. (1991). *Everyone can win: How to resolve conflict.* Sydney, Australia: Simon & Schuster.

Davis, B. L., Gebelein, S. H., Hellervik, L. W., Sheard, J. L., & Skube, C. J. (1992). *The successful manager's handbook: Development suggestions for today's managers.* Minneapolis: Personnel Decisions, Inc.

Drury, S. S. (1984). *Assertive supervision: Building involved teamwork.* Champaign, IL: Research Press.

Ellis, A., & Harper, R. (1975). *A guide to rational living.* North Hollywood, CA: Wilshire.

Ferraro, V. L., & Adams, S. A. (1984). Interdepartmental conflict: Practical ways to prevent and reduce it. *Personnel, 61,* 12-23.

Fisher, R., & Brown, S. (1988). *Getting together: Building a relationship that gets to yes.* Boston: Houghton Mifflin.

Fisher, R., & Stone, D. (1990). *Working it out: A handbook on negotiation for high school students.* Cambridge, MA: Harvard Program on Negotiation.

Fisher, R., & Ury, W. (1981). *Getting to yes: Negotiating agreement without giving in.* New York: Penguin.

Goldberg, S. B., Green, E. D., & Snider, F. (1987, July). Saying you're sorry. *Negotiation Journal,* 221-223.

Hall, L. (Ed.). (1993). *Negotiation: Strategies for mutual gain.* Newbury Park: Sage.

Hankins, G., & Hankins, C. (1993). *Prescription for anger: Coping with angry feelings and angry people.* New York: Warner Books.

Ilich, J., & Jones, B. S. (1981). *Successful negotiating skills for women.* Reading, MA: Addison-Wesley.

Lax, D. A., & Sebenius, J. K. (1986). *The manager as negotiator: Bargaining for cooperation and competitive gain.* New York: Free Press.

Morris, C., & Pirie, A. (Eds.). (1994). *Qualifications for dispute resolution: Perspectives on the debate.* Victoria, BC: UVIC Institute for Dispute Resolution.

Nierenberg, G. (1971). *Creative business negotiating.* New York: Hawthorn.

Nierenberg, G. (1973). *Fundamentals of negotiating.* New York: Hawthorn.

Nierenberg, G. (1986). *The complete negotiator.* New York: Nierenberg & Zeif.

Pruitt, D., & Rubin, J. (1986). *Social conflict: Escalation, stalemate, and settlement.* New York: Random House.

Rackham, N. (1984). *The psychology of negotiating* (Listen & Learn Tape No. T35). (Available from Listen & Learn Cassettes, Box 344 Station M, Toronto, Ontario, M6S 4T6, Canada)

Raiffa, H. (1982). *The art and science of negotiation.* Cambridge, MA: Harvard University Press.

Robinson, F. P. (1970). *Effective study* (4th ed.). New York: Harper & Row.

Rubin, J. Z., & Rubin, C. (1989). *When families fight: How to handle conflict with those you love.* New York: Ballantine.

Russo, J. E., & Schoemaker, P. J. H. (1989). *Decision traps: The ten barriers to brilliant decision-making and how to overcome them.* New York: Doubleday.

Schoonmaker, A. (1989). *Negotiate to win: Gaining the psychological edge.* Englewood Cliffs, NJ: Prentice Hall.

Spencer, L. M., Jr.., & Spencer, S. M. (1993). *Competence at work: Models for superior performance.* New York: John Wiley.

Sternberg, R. J., & Wagner, R. K. (Eds.). (1986). *Practical intelligence: Nature and origins of competence in the everyday world.* New York: Cambridge University Press.

Stone, D. C. (1991). *Building bridges: A high school curriculum on negotiation.* Cambridge, MA: Harvard Program on Negotiation.

Susskind, L., & Cruikshank, J. (1988). *Breaking the impasse: Consensual approaches to resolving public disputes.* New York: Basic Books.

Thompson, G., & Stroud, M. (1984). *Verbal judo: Redirecting behavior with words.* Albuquerque, NM: Communication Strategies, Inc.

Ury, W. (1991). *Getting past no: Dealing with difficult people.* New York: Bantam.

Ury, W. L., Brett, J. M., & Goldberg, S. B. (1993). *Getting disputes resolved: Designing systems to cut the costs of conflict.* Cambridge, MA: Harvard Program on Negotiation.

Walther, G. R. (1986). *Phone power: How to make the telephone your most profitable business tool.* New York: G. P. Putnam.

Watson, D. L., & Tharp, R. G. (1977). *Self-directed behavior: Self-modification for personal adjustment* (2nd ed.). Belmont, CA: Wadsworth.

Williams, G. R. (1983). *Legal negotiation and settlement.* St. Paul, MN: West.

Williams, G. R. (1993). Style and effectiveness in negotiation. In L. Hall (Ed.), *Negotiation: Strategies for mutual gain.* Newbury Park, CA: Sage.

Zemke, R. (1985). The Honeywell studies: How managers learn to manage. *Training, 22,* 46-51.

# Index

■  ■  ■  ■

# About the Author

■ ■ ■ ■

**Brad McRae** is the president of McRae and Associates. He holds a doctoral degree in counseling psychology from the University of British Columbia and is a registered psychologist, a consultant, and an author. He has taught at the British Columbia Institute of Technology and at Carleton University in Ottawa and has lectured across Canada and in the United States, Mexico, and Africa. He was trained in negotiating skills at Harvard University's Program on Negotiation and is a member of the National Speakers Association.

He gives more than 100 presentations a year on such topics as stress management, time management, dealing with difficult people, effective negotiating and influencing skills, maintaining peak performance, managing change and uncertainty, and exceptional customer service. He has written *How to Write a Thesis and Keep Your Sanity, Executive Health: A Self-Management Approach to a Healthier Lifestyle,* and the Canadian bestseller *Practical Time Management: How to Get More Done in Less Time.*